A DISTANT Prayer

A DISTANT *Prayer*

MIRACLES OF THE 49TH COMBAT MISSION

Joseph Banks
and
Jerry Borrowman

Covenant Communications, Inc.

Covenant

Published by Covenant Communications, Inc.
American Fork, Utah

Printed in Canada
First Printing: October 2001

08 07 06 05 04 03 02   10 9 8 7 6 5 4

ISBN 1-57734-905-9

Library of Congress Cataloging-in-Publication Data

Banks, Joseph, 1923-
    A distant prayer / Joseph Banks, Jerry Borrowman.
      p. cm.
    Includes bibliographical references.
    ISBN 1-57734-905-9
    1. Banks, Joseph, 1923-   . 2. World War, 1939-1945--Personal narratives, American. 3. United States. Army Air Forces--Biography. 4. Flight engineers--United States--Biography. 5. B-17 bomber. 6. World War, 1939-1945--Prisoners and prisons, German. 7. Prisoners of war--United States--Biography. 8. Mormons--United States--Biography.
    I. Borrowman, Jerry. II. Title.
    D811.B3315 A3 2001
    940.54'7243'092--dc21   2001042299

*This book is dedicated
to my fallen crewmates and fellow prisoners,
who sacrificed their lives in the cause of freedom.*

ACKNOWLEDGEMENTS

We wish to acknowledge all those who contributed to the writing of this book. Many reviewed the script as it was being written and edited, and their feedback was invaluable. We'd particularly like to thank Bob Dodge, a former Vietnam War pilot who reviewed the book for technical accuracy and Steve Jensen, who illustrated the B-17 aircraft. We especially appreciate Afton Banks and Marcella Borrowman, our wives, for their encouragement and for the many hours they spent reading and critiquing the work.

TABLE OF CONTENTS

FOREWORD

Joseph Banks, a young American combat airman, left the tranquility, security, and love of his home in Utah to serve his country during the dark days of World War II. Throughout all the ordeals that Joe endured, including the horrors of his 49th mission over Europe, when he was the lone survivor of the crew of his B-17 bomber, Joe was sustained by his faith in God and his country, his resolute determination to remain true to the tenets and teachings of his religion, and his deep love for his wife, Afton, and their infant son, Randy.

I am Joe's brother, Ben. Though I was only a boy when the events portrayed in this book occurred, I understood enough even then to know that Joe, like so many thousands of others, was a true American hero. He remains so for me today. I admire his physical courage, but even more, I admire his integrity, which never wavered, even in the face of danger, privation, loneliness, despair, and temptations of modern war.

Elder Ben Banks
The Presidency of the Seventy
Salt Lake City, Utah
October, 2000

CHAPTER 1

Airborne!

It was almost a relief when the bugler sounded reveille at 0600 hours. I had been awake most of the night, anxiously awaiting the dawn of day when I would take my first flight in an airplane. Having grown up in Salt Lake City, Utah, during the impoverished years of the Great Depression, I had never imagined that a moment like this would come. Yet here I was in Long Beach, California, in the summer of 1943, having spent the previous six weeks studying a B-17 bomber bolt by bolt as part of my training to become a combat flight engineer. Words are inadequate to describe the anticipation I felt in contemplating that first flight aboard a single-engine military-training aircraft. My feelings were a combination of excitement and anxiety, particularly since it was one of my team's training assignments to disassemble the engine of the aircraft I was about to board, and then reassemble it piece by piece. Assembly tolerances had to be perfect for the powerful Curtiss Wright engine to perform in flight. Fortunately, we had been taught to systematically check every procedure multiple times, knowing that our very lives depended on it.

After breakfast my teammates and I gathered in one of the hangars to await our turn in the air, chatting nervously while waiting to hear our names called. At last, I heard the rather bored, metallic voice on the public address system instruct me to proceed to the flight-line where the aircraft waited. As I gave the guys a thumbs-up and started out onto the field, I found myself staring straight ahead while walking in the vicinity of the other aircraft on the tarmac. The memory of a horrifying experience my crew and I had witnessed just a few days earlier was still fresh in my mind. Before anyone could realize what was happening, another trainee had walked straight into the huge spinning propeller blades of a P-38 fighter aircraft. He made the mistake of focusing on the whirling propeller, which can create a mesmerizing effect. His death left everyone sick and frightened.

As I reached our assigned aircraft, I forced thoughts of the incident from my mind and climbed aboard to assume my position next to the pilot, who had wedged himself in the cockpit and was busy going through the preflight checklist. My role on this flight was mostly as a passenger, although the pilot asked me to monitor the engine gauges on the control panel. It was at this point that my anxiety was greatest, for in just a few moments our work in the shop would be put to the test when the engine was started as part of the preflight test. The pilot firmly commanded, "Start engine!" I confirmed the "props clear" item on the checklist and then engaged the starter. Wow! My heart was pounding. I heard the distinctive sound of the compressed-air canister propelling the engine to starting rpm, and listened intently as I watched the engine belch a cloud of black smoke from its exhaust caused by the rich fuel mixture used in starting. The engine sputtered and choked until it was idling harmoniously, waiting for the pilot to unleash its tremendous power. I think it was the most wonderful sound I had ever heard. A failure would have washed my entire training crew out of the program.

The pilot took control of the aircraft and eased the throttles forward. My heart rate seemed to increase along with the accelerating revolutions of the aircraft engine. I wasn't really frightened about the performance of the aircraft anymore because the run-up checklist was completed successfully. I was just excited to experience flight. Slowly the aircraft lumbered across the runway to the assigned position for takeoff. When he was cleared by the control tower, the pilot applied full throttle, and the engine roared to life with such force that the developing acceleration pushed us back against our seats. As the aircraft gained airspeed I realized that I was moving faster than at any other time in my life. During acceleration the runway imperfections were transmitted through the airframe to our seats in an ever-increasing crescendo. Suddenly the aircraft gracefully lifted off the ground and we were airborne.

The sensation of flight was better than anything I could have ever imagined. We seemed to float above the ground. I marveled at how the golden hills of southern California looked from this perspective, and gasped as we banked out over the ocean. I wanted this feeling to last forever.

Unfortunately, there wasn't much time to enjoy the view. Just moments after takeoff the pilot was instructed to re-enter the traffic pattern for landing. This was, after all, a training mission, not a tourist excursion. The aircraft descended towards the ground and touched the runway with a distinct, jarring thud. As we taxied off the runway I could hardly believe it was over. I thought it strange that my personal view of the world could change so much in such a short time. Just a few hours earlier I had been anxious and nervous, wondering if I'd measure up to the challenge of flight. Now I couldn't wait for my next opportunity to go up. Rather than being frightened by the experience, I was exhilarated at the knowledge that as long as I had to take part in World War II, at least I could do it in the company of my crewmates in the United States Army Air Force.

CHAPTER 2

Entering the Battle

As a young boy I had always looked forward to the chance to serve a mission for my Church in some far-off corner of the world, particularly after my brother Berry spent two and a half years in Argentina. But in 1939, when I was sixteen years old, the political situation in Europe and Asia deteriorated to the point that the First Presidency announced that they would no longer issue new mission calls. That was just one of the ways that Germany's Chancellor, Adolf Hitler, interfered in the lives of ordinary people all around the world. The wisdom of the First Presidency's decision was manifest. War broke out in Europe in the fall of 1939. With the government's announcement a few months later that all males age eighteen and older would have to register with the Selective Service, I knew that whatever plans I had before the war would have to wait until it was over.

While no one wanted America to be drawn into another war, the conflict in Europe did help the country shake off the high unemployment of the Great Depression. President Roosevelt declared that America should be the "Arsenal of Democracy," which put people to work manufacturing war materiel´ to sell to Britain and her allies. In 1941 I was fortunate to obtain a job in a war-related industry when I was hired as a clerk by the Union Pacific Railroad. Prior to that I'd been an auto mechanic for a small garage on State Street in Salt Lake City. The war had a more direct impact on my girlfriend, Afton, who had worked for tips and a small hourly wage at a drive-in restaurant when I first met her. With the outbreak of war she was hired to work for a munitions factory making artillery shells at a higher wage than I earned at the railroad.

When the Japanese bombed Pearl Harbor in December 1941, I was eighteen years old, just old enough to be considered for military service. A call to service was not automatic at that point since I worked in a war-related industry. Afton was the main reason I held back, since our relationship was getting pretty serious. We decided to wait and see how things developed. By mid-1942 it was obvious that the war was not going well for the Allies, and the chances of a general call to service increased daily. I talked it over with Afton and we decided that regardless of what the future held, we wanted to share it with each other. Though we were still young, she accepted my proposal of marriage. We were married in the Salt Lake Temple in September 1942.

Starting a life together while worrying that I'd be drafted was very stressful. Sometimes we'd fret and stew about it; other times we ignored it, pretending that things would always stay as they were at that time. Neither approach worked very well.

Six months after our marriage the mailman brought the letter we dreaded. Dated March 1943, it began, "Greetings, you have been selected to serve in the Armed Forces of the United States." I had so many mixed emotions. On the one hand, I wanted to serve my country in what was quickly becoming the most ferocious war ever fought. I knew that freedom required sacrifice, particularly from young men my age. But on the other hand, the thought of leaving Afton was almost overpowering, particularly since we'd learned two months earlier that she was expecting our first child. How could I leave them? We both sat down and cried for a while, then went next door to tell my widowed mother the news. I'm sure that a similar scene was played out in millions of homes across the country as the United States geared itself to wage a full-scale war in both Europe and the Pacific.

For the next eighteen months I was in training. I was fortunate to go to Basic Training in Kearns, Utah, just a half hour drive from our home in Salt Lake City. It was a very grueling experience in which they tried to break down each person's individuality in order to turn us into a fighting unit. Fortunately, I enjoyed athletics and that made it easier for me to endure the rigorous physical training. Some of the less physically fit men broke down and washed out of combat service.

Being close to home meant that Afton could come pick me up for weekend leave on a number of occasions. It was always so great to go home and visit her and my other relatives. For a few hours I was able to relax and feel like my old civilian self again, secure in the presence of familiar surroundings and people. We'd always time my arrival back at camp so that I could walk through the gates at the latest moment possible, 11:59 p.m.

Toward the end of Basic Training everyone waited anxiously to find out where they'd be assigned to serve, such as infantry or artillery. I was shocked when they told me I was going to be a medic; I'd never had any interest in medicine. I loved anything to do with mechanics, and had assumed I'd do something related to that. But the army doesn't give you a choice, so I spent several weeks learning basic first aid and how to provide initial help to seriously wounded men. In spite of my previous inexperience, I found that I had the "stomach" for this kind of service, and my instructors said I might actually have some aptitude for it.

I was still relieved, however, when an officer called me in one day to tell me that after reviewing my aptitude test scores, they were reassigning me to the Army Air Forces as a flight engineer. That was something to get excited about! All the hours I'd spent working on the engine of my powerful old 1932 Chrysler might pay off after all.

I first went to Long Beach, California, for engineering school, then to Kingman, Arizona, for weapons training, and finally to Dyersburg, Tennessee, for Flight School. It was there that I was assigned to my permanent flight crew. We trained on the famed B-17 "Flying Fortress" bomber, the backbone of the military effort in Europe. I came to love this machine. As the engineer, I acted as the in-flight mechanic who was responsible for the operation of the four 1200 horsepower supercharged Wright R-1820-97 Cyclone rotary engines, as well as the other hydraulic, mechanical, and life support systems that made the aircraft such a remarkable weapon.

Even greater than my affection for the aircraft, however, was the feeling of brotherhood I developed with the nine other men on our crew. For nearly a year we trained together practically around the clock, learning to fly both daylight and nighttime missions in all kinds of weather conditions. Even though we came from all parts of the country, with very different feelings about religion, politics, and our ultimate career ambitions, we learned to work together as a team and to care about how the others were feeling. The B-17 has the following complement:

Pilot
Copilot
Bombardier
Navigator
Engineer
Radio Operator
Left & Right Waist Gunners
Tail Gunner
Lower Ball Turret Gunner

The pilot, copilot, bombardier, and navigator always stayed at their special assignment, but the rest of us rotated through the different positions so we could back each other up in combat.[1]

The following were some of the men with whom I served.

Ron Tonkovich, our pilot, was the aircraft commander. He had ultimate authority over the rest of the crew, and was the one who would make on-the-spot decisions about a mission (such as to abort because of damage, or to proceed in spite of difficulties). He was a quiet young man who didn't talk a lot but who loved to read. Tonk, as we called him, had blond hair, a slender build, and was fairly short in stature. From talking with him, we learned that he was engaged to be married when he arrived home. Nothing seemed to rattle him, even when someone on the crew messed up. He'd just take us through the procedure again until everyone had it down pat.

Dick LoPriesti, our copilot, was a person who was in high gear all the time. He had lots of nervous energy that kept him in constant motion. Dick loved to talk to people, and he was always the life of the party. He was very slim and much taller than either Ron or me. He'd get pretty excited when something went wrong, but could be counted on to do his part. Dick was single and never talked about a special girl back home.

"Batch" Batcheler was our bombardier. He liked to egg us on in an argument, although it was always for fun. He was a happy person who loved to tell jokes, although he always started laughing before he got the punch line out. Batch had a hot temper that he worked hard to control. He was six feet tall and a bit pudgy in places. When we were on a mission he always had a story to tell to relax us a bit, and I looked forward to hearing his voice come over the interphone, even though he liked to pepper his phrases with profanity. Since he was positioned in the Plexiglas nosecone of the aircraft, I always thought he had the best view in the world, with a nearly 180 degree field of vision open before him. Batch was an avowed atheist who often challenged my religious faith, but never in a mean-spirited way.

Our navigator, whose name I cannot recall, was a super guy who was extremely competent at his work. He was about the same height as Batch, but quite slim. Throughout the mission he was careful to give us updates on our progress to and from the objective, which helped ease the tension. He was always concerned about the other members of the crew, and would frequently ask if he could help us.

Tom Hurd was our radio operator. He was a worrier who often brooded over things. Tom loved his "Southern Comfort" whiskey and liked to tell and listen to jokes, particularly after a few drinks. He had a steady girlfriend back home that he talked about now and then.

Tom Hynes was one of the waist gunners and the tallest member of the crew. Tom was going bald and was really touchy when kidded about it. He had a strong New Jersey accent and a quick temper. He was married and had a son that he talked about and missed deeply. I could tell that he was a good father. I was always amazed at Tom's skill in telling jokes in rapid-fire succession without pausing or even missing a beat. I think he was the oldest member of our crew.

Mike, our other waist gunner, had a slight build and quick reactions. He was a nervous chain smoker who used profanity often, which bothered me since I didn't like to use swear words. But he would willingly give you the shirt off his back if he thought you needed it. Even though Mike had never been to engineering school he loved the aircraft and learned everything he could about it. Sometimes he'd help me with the preflight inspection, or change places with me during the flight to keep things more interesting.

Our tail gunner, Jack Cook, was from the south. He had the most drawn-out drawl I've ever heard. It seemed to take him forever to say something. Jack loved good liquor, cigars, and cigarettes, and could always be counted on to have a funny story to tell when the mood got too serious for his liking. He was a fighter who would step in to defend us if anybody on our crew ever got into trouble with other servicemen. Jack had a lot of experience with women and liked to tell the stories of his exploits over and over again. That bothered me a lot, but my discomfort didn't dissuade Jack at all.

Shorty Krasnouskie was our lower ball turret gunner, and was the shortest and smallest member of the crew—he had to be to fit in the turret. Shorty would get pretty nervous down in the turret, and sometimes said he wanted to come out to "get some air," but he never once left his station, even during the hottest moments of combat. Shorty loved the opera, classical music, and reading. He blushed whenever anyone told a shady joke (he frequently had a red face). He had a steady girlfriend back home and liked to tell us about going to the opera or ballet with her. Unfortunately, none of the rest of us knew anything about the arts so we couldn't really share his excitement. Shorty had a wonderful vocabulary, and was very interesting to talk to.

It's remarkable how easily we formed close friendships in spite of our differences. Perhaps it was because our lives would depend on each other when we went into combat.

I was fortunate to have Afton join me in Dyersberg, Tennessee, for the last few months of training. This was wonderful for us, even though it was hard for her to leave our son back home with my mother. Randy had been born while I was in engineering school, and the army had given me a special leave to return home to give him a name and a blessing. I was grateful for the chance to see him before receiving a combat assignment. It was wonderful to live as husband and wife during those few weeks together, taking strolls through the small Tennessee town, enjoying dinner together at a local diner, and dropping in on area churches on Sunday to enjoy the singing and spirit of friendship that the local people showered on the "boys in the military."

We would talk for hours about our feelings for one another and our plans for after the war. When the time came for Afton to board the Greyhound Bus for her trip back to Salt Lake City, my heart ached as it pulled away from the curb and Afton put her head out the window to wave to me one last time. This time it was a permanent good-bye, and neither of us knew if we'd see each other again. The only thing that sustained me was the remembrance of kneeling together in earnest prayer in our small apartment, asking the Lord to somehow preserve our lives so that we could see each other again. The warm feeling of the Spirit had given us the impression that somehow things would work out, but we didn't know if it would be in this life or after death.

The next transfer took my crewmates and me to Norfolk, Virginia, where we boarded a troop transport for Europe. After nearly a year of training, it was with mixed feelings that I stood at the railing of the ship as we pulled away from the dock, watching as America slowly disappeared from view. I was excited to see new places and face the challenge of combat after so much practice. But it was 1943 and the war with Germany was intensifying. The casualty rate for air combat crews was so high that the odds of our crew making it back in one piece were very slim.

Most of the voyage was pretty boring, with nothing to do but sit around and speculate whether we were going to Africa or Europe. It did get pretty exciting, however, when our convoy came under attack by enemy submarines. Our ship was part of a large, high-speed troop convoy that provided a lot of tempting targets for the German U-Boats. Fortunately, there was a strong escort of powerful cruisers and destroyers that prowled about nervously to protect us. They could easily outrun any enemy submarine or, for that matter, any ship in the convoy. When the first warning bells sounded, indicating that the enemy had launched an attack on one of the other troop ships, we watched as our escorts poured on the steam to engage the submarines in battle. Their absence left us feeling vulnerable and alone. I could occasionally hear the sound of the big guns firing off in the distance, and feel the concussions of the depth charges going off in the ocean. Even though our ship was well behind the scene of battle, the under-water explosions reverberated through the hull until it felt like we'd be blown out of the ocean along with the enemy. I could only imagine the horror of being a German sailor on the submarines under attack.

After two weeks of wondering and guessing where we were going, the officers finally told us that we would arrive in Oran, North Africa, in just two more days. Passing under the imposing Rock of Gibraltar was an amazing experience because it conjured up a sense of mystery and adventure in my imagination. I could hardly believe that I was about to disembark in Africa. To me, this was a land of fable and myth. I probably should have been more anxious about going into combat, but after eighteen months of training we were fairly excited to see some real action. I'm sure the fresh, idealistic-looking expressions on our faces provided some real amusement to the battle-experienced crews that saw us at a briefing the next morning. They knew that it wouldn't be long before the excitement would give way to the desperation inevitable in air combat, where the only conscious objective was to make it out alive.

After flying several training missions from our base in Africa, we learned that our first combat mission would take us to Italy. Our objective there was to damage an aircraft manufacturing factory. I'll never forget that first day. After breakfast my crew and I returned to our tents to retrieve our flight gear, which consisted of a parachute, heated flight suit, leather helmet, silk liner gloves and insulated flight gloves. Since the B-17 was a flying battle fortress with weapons protruding out of multiple openings in the fuselage, the aircraft could not be pressurized. At high altitudes the air was bitter cold (with a wind chill factor of −50 degrees centigrade at some altitudes). A man's skin could freeze in a matter of moments if exposed to the outside air. By the time we were fully suited we looked like explorers setting out on an Arctic expedition. The air was also very thin at our typical cruising altitude of 25,000 feet, which required everyone to wear oxygen masks. The masks took some getting used to. The hoses that connected the mask to the oxygen supply essentially tethered us to our position, limiting our ability to move easily about the aircraft. It was cumbersome to disconnect from the main oxygen system and connect to a portable tank when one of us had to move to another position. The bulky flight suit, the oxygen mask, and heavy gloves made our operational tasks even more challenging.

As the flight engineer it was my responsibility to complete a preflight checklist of the aircraft and the onboard systems before each mission. Once that was complete, the members of the crew boarded the aircraft, checked their own area for operational readiness, then moved to the radio room where we waited for take-off.

Words are inadequate to describe the physical and emotional sensation created by the sound, smells, and sight of nearly a hundred military aircraft preparing to launch into action against the enemy.

Exhaust fumes filled the hot desert air as our small armada revved their engines in preparation for flight. When cleared for take-off, the throttles were "pushed to the wall" to develop maximum power for a short take-off roll before lift off.

Once airborne, the crew assumed battle positions, connected their electric flight suits and oxygen masks, and prepared their weapons for action. Small talk was exchanged over the interphone. At 10,000 feet the pilot instructed us to don our oxygen masks and test our weapons. Several rounds of ammo were expended from each weapon, with particular caution to avoid a sister aircraft.

My assignment as flight engineer required me to fulfill the dual roles of both maintaining the aircraft in flight and manning the upper turret machine gun to defend against attacks from enemy fighter aircraft diving from above. The weapons in my turret extended nearly two feet outside of the Plexiglas canopy to allow the muzzle blasts to safely dissipate without damage to our own aircraft. I could rotate the turret 360 degrees in the horizontal plane and aim the weapon above the horizon to engage the enemy aircraft. One of the disadvantages of this position was that I could not depress the weapon's line of fire below the horizon, or it would hit our own aircraft. German fighters would capitalize on this limitation by matching our altitude exactly while approaching from the 12:00 position (directly head on), so that only the nose gunners' weapons could be brought to bear. It was the game of "chicken" at a combined airspeed of over 600 miles per hour! To maintain formation, our aircraft fired on the intruder, but did not take evasive action, so the approaching fighter had to sheer off at the last possible moment to avoid a collision.

Once we checked our weapons and reported on our individual operational readiness, everyone was pretty much left to their own thoughts. It was quite lonely and monotonous while flying toward the objective. Periodically the navigator advised us of our position enroute to the target, and the estimated time of arrival. We could also monitor his communication with the pilot as he provided headings to be entered into the navigational equipment. In between these stilted conversations, my thoughts wandered to home and I found myself praying that no one would be hurt on the mission, and that we would get back to base safely. I also prayed that I would have the courage to do my duty.

I was particularly anxious on our first mission. It would be the first time I might have to fire a gun at another human being in an attempt to destroy his life, and I fretted about it. What I didn't realize at the time was that when the enemy starts firing, something goes off in the mind and one fights back furiously out of a sense of self-preservation. Raw emotion takes over, and reactions to the battle are without conscious thought or remorse.

Regardless of whatever I was thinking at the time, I was almost always startled by the voice of the navigator telling us we had crossed into enemy territory. At that point, everyone on board began straining his eyes to see any sign of enemy fighters. We initiated an assigned drill of periodically confirming our condition so that if someone were injured or killed without getting word to us, we would quickly find out if something was wrong.

The noise of combat is unlike anything in human experience, with the drone of the engines, the screaming sound of fighter aircraft whizzing past at an airspeed of over three hundred miles-per-hour, the rapid fire bursts from the twelve machine guns mounted throughout the ship, and perhaps worst of all, the constant pounding of the Triple A (Anti-Aircraft Artillery) exploding all around. I'll never forget the first time we passed over an area where the Italians fired Triple A at our aircraft. I saw the distinctive puffs of black smoke in the distance, indicating that the enemy had fired flak shells from their ground-based anti-aircraft artillery. Flak is metal shrapnel that is designed to tear an aircraft to pieces when the projectile that carries it explodes near the aircraft at a pre-determined altitude. Flak shells were always fired in groups of three, and we had been trained to watch how the pattern developed. If the second puff was further away than the first, we knew that the ground guns didn't have our range. If the second shot was closer than the first, then it was time to hope that they hadn't guessed our altitude because the third shot was likely to explode very close to our position. Even a near-hit was sometimes enough to destroy an aircraft, since the effect of flying into flak is much like walking into the whirling blades of a table saw. Shrapnel can penetrate the metal skin of an aircraft like a can opener cutting a tin can. A direct hit would rip entire sections off a wing or the fuselage, tearing the aircraft's aluminum skin into razor-sharp strands that could slice through a flight suit, or even a person's skin if he accidentally touched it. If the flak was set to explode at altitudes above our assigned altitude, there was a risk that a well-aimed projectile would tear a hole right through the aircraft on its upward trajectory. It didn't do any good for us to shoot back at the ground based artillery, since we typically flew at altitudes in excess of 15,000 to 20,000 feet, placing the enemy guns far beyond the range of our .50 caliber machine guns.

One of the most frustrating things about serving on a bomber is the inability to take any offensive action. We always flew in squadrons that required us to maintain formation, regardless of what the enemy Triple A or fighters were doing to us. It was unnerving to watch a German fighter approaching at over three hundred miles-per-hour, knowing that we could not take any evasive action to get out of their way. The reasons were that a bomber was too large to maneuver quickly, and we also had to maintain our position or risk crashing into one of our own aircraft just a few feet to either side. We were forced to use the twelve .50 caliber machine guns that protruded from our aircraft as our only defense. Of course at the speed we were traveling, (approximately two hundred miles-per-hour), it was rare that we'd ever hit an enemy fighter—we could only hope to force them off course so they couldn't get a good fix on our position. It was unnerving to think that another person was trying his best to kill you, and it soon stripped away any sense of excitement we might have held when we first arrived in the combat zone.

Since enemy fighters can swarm a single aircraft and attack until it's destroyed, we always flew in squadrons. Upwards of twenty-five or more four-aircraft groups combined to create a squadron. By flying in a four-aircraft formation, an approaching enemy fighter was confronted not by twelve defensive weapons, but by four times that many, which made their job a lot tougher. It also afforded each aircraft in the group additional protection. The lead aircraft in each formation flew in the forward position with one aircraft to each side and a little behind in the left wing and right wing positions. These three flew at the same altitude and were so close to each other that we could easily see each other's faces when peering out of our Plexiglas windows. The fourth aircraft flew behind the two in wing positions in a direct line behind the lead aircraft. This position was called the Tail

End Charlie. Charlie flew at a somewhat lower altitude. Since the most vulnerable positions were the lead and tail, we took turns flying in each of the four positions so that each crew had equal exposure to danger. Each position had its own peculiar dangers, but the least popular, by far, was the tail end position.

The advantage of flying in a squadron was that we didn't feel so alone. The bad part was that we were so close to each other that if one of the aircraft got hit, we'd all feel the concussion created by the explosion. It made us sick to our stomachs thinking about the men who had just been killed. Sometimes we'd see parachutes, which was a cause for celebration. If we were still in friendly airspace our radio operator could call out coordinates to help effect a rescue. In enemy territory the navigator recorded the position so we could call it in when we got back to Allied airspace. We had to maintain radio silence in enemy territory, since any electronic noise could give the enemy artillery crews a fixed bead on our position.

At the instant the bombardier called out "Bombs Away!" almost everyone on board shouted in unison, "Let's get out of here!" and the pilot would bank to the left or right based on a pre-determined flight path that kept the formation together. We never broke ranks unless an aircraft was destroyed or severely damaged by enemy fire, and then the following aircraft had to move forward and take its position. When casualties were particularly high, the entire squadron reshuffled itself periodically to stay in close formation so we could offer the greatest resistance to enemy fighters on the way home.

The ground crew always knew in advance the distance to be traveled, and they fueled the aircraft accordingly. On really long flights they topped off the tanks, but sometimes it simply wasn't enough. On more than one occasion an aircraft had to ditch or crash land because it ran out of fuel. Sometimes it went down over water, which increased the danger of casualties considerably. The most frustrating part of a mission to me came when we were almost clear of enemy territory only to encounter a flak unit in some small little town that threw up a barrage of Triple A. Although the chance of being damaged by these isolated units was remote, I remember on one occasion flying over a small city that had just three guns firing. Yet sure enough, one of them hit the lead aircraft and the crew had to bail out. It made us all sick to think that they'd gone all the way to the target, dropped their bombs, and had almost made it back to friendly territory only to go down.

Because the fighter aircraft were too small to carry the fuel needed to fly all the way to most objectives, they almost always had to return to base long before we made it to the target. Once they were gone, the enemy fighters would swarm in, since we were flying into their territory and range. It was a lonely and anxious moment when our fighters broke off on the outbound leg of a mission, and a huge relief when they joined us on the trip home. We started to relax a little bit. Then, as the Adriatic came into view, the lead aircraft peeled off, followed by the right wing, the left wing, and finally Tail End Charlie.

As our descending altitude dropped to ten thousand feet, the outside air started to warm up, and there was enough natural oxygen that we could breathe without the help of an oxygen mask. Everyone stripped off his oxygen mask to enjoy the freedom of breathing on his own, and then we moved to the radio room for landing.

Once we were safely on the ground, there wasn't a lot to do. There were no shows or other recreation. We'd usually go over to the PX and have a glass of beer or Coke while talking to each other. A lot of the men played cards or tossed a football back and forth.

As the only member of The Church of Jesus Christ of Latter-day Saints in the entire camp, I often stood out from the rest of the group, particularly since I abstained from alcohol and tobacco. At first I felt self-conscious about it, but pretty soon most people came to accept and even admire the standards I lived by. My crewmates would stand up for me if anyone ever teased me or tried to convince me to compromise my standards. While some of the men escaped the stress of battle through immoral behavior, I managed to resist temptation by fixing my mind on the goal of returning home to Afton, worthy to return with her to the temple.

Some of the men in camp came to view me as a chaplain, and they'd come to see me for advice on a personal problem or to settle a dispute. While I didn't try to draw attention to myself, there were times when even the most hardened of men needed to talk about spiritual concerns. I always took time to hear these people out and to try and help them resolve their problems. I was sometimes amazed at how many of the men told me that they didn't really have anyone at home they could confide in or turn to for support. This helped me understand how blessed I was to have a whole family and neighborhood praying for me back in Utah. I always promised the men that I would remember them in my prayers, and I think it offered some of them comfort. On many occasions, in the heat of battle, other members of the crew would ask me to say a prayer through the interphone system, although that sometimes led to gentle ridicule from the bombardier, our self-proclaimed atheist.

From our base in North Africa we flew combat missions to Italy and Southern Germany. About a month after arriving in Africa, we were transferred to Foggia, Italy, to take advantage of the forward position gained by our ground troops. Our new base gave us the opportunity to strike deep into the heart of Germany, taking out war production factories as well as the fuel refineries in Rumania. It also increased the danger dramatically, since the German defenders were more highly skilled, better equipped, and more motivated to protect their homeland than the Italians had been. In fact, because many of the Italians had hoped to be liberated by the Allies to get out from under the Mussolini dictatorship, they only put up token resistance. But the Nazis were far more disciplined, and could always be counted on to create a fierce defense.

The worst assignment was to bomb the Nazi oil refineries in Ploesti, Rumania. The best way to describe it is as a scene out of Dante's *Inferno*. I'm sure that even the most imaginative vision of hell can't exceed the horror of flying into Ploesti, where the black flak clouds were so thick it felt like we were flying into a deadly fog. When our bombs blew up an oil storage tank, the flames would leap high into the air while black smoke billowed up to obscure our approach.

As the number of missions started to add up, the stress of battle became almost unbearable. One of our crewmates, Tom Hurd, the radio operator, became deathly ill each time we passed ten thousand feet, and eventually received a medical discharge because he just couldn't face the emotional challenge of going into battle anymore. The rest of us stayed at our assignments, but I noticed that my hands would tremble after each mission, when I had time to sit on my cot and think about what we'd been through.

An aircrew in our theatre of operations was required to complete twenty-five missions before they could be reassigned from the combat zone to training responsibilities in the States. There was no one better qualified to teach the responsibilities of each position on the aircraft than those who had lived through actual combat missions. Yet by the time we arrived, the number of required missions had increased to fifty. The mortality rate was so high that they just couldn't bring in new crews fast enough, so the number of required missions was extended to keep experienced crews in service. Fifty missions is an unbelievable number; with such a high injury and kill rate it almost wasn't worth keeping track.

The pace was incredible. After just three months in combat, we had gone on more than forty missions. That made us the senior veterans that the new guys looked up to in awe. It's still hard for me to believe we survived some of the raids we went on, given the damage we had received from flak and attacks by enemy fighter aircraft. Yet somehow the missions added up and we were still together and flying.

It was amazing how much my life had changed in less than two years. I'd gone from a kid who liked working on automobiles and playing football at West High School to a seasoned engineer on a beat-up B-17 bomber. Now that we were getting close to fifty missions, I sometimes let myself think about what it would be like to go back home to the States where I could work as an engineering instructor during the day, and return home to my wife and son at night.

I wanted so desperately to get out of the Italian battle zone, where the civilian economy had been devastated by the destruction of the war, where boys like me were turned into violent killers, and where the threat of permanent disability or death was ever-present. I watched so many friends from other crews being sent home in ambulances it left me almost numb. I couldn't wait to get back to a normal life.

It was about this time that I had an experience that struck me as being symbolic of everything that had gone wrong in a world turned upside down by war. While taking a walk with two of my buddies through Foggia, Italy, we came across a small boy leaning against a tree. He couldn't have been more than eight years old, and he was standing there with his right leg and an arm missing. He balanced himself with a stick, and asked if we had any food or money. I went over to him, knelt down, and quietly asked what had happened to him. Since he'd spoken English to request help, I thought he might be able to tell me his story. In broken English and with a few painful gestures, he indicated that he had stepped on a land mine. I had witnessed wounds and injuries far worse than this, but all of a sudden I found myself sobbing, almost uncontrollably. When I regained my composure I gave him all the cash I had and asked if he'd like me to carry him home. He said no and thanked me as I wiped the tears off my face. Many times since then I've remembered the image of this little boy leaning against the tree with a pitiful look on his face, and I've wept for all the children who suffer because of the dreadful decisions of adults. I went back to my tent that night and offered a prayer on his behalf. With more than forty missions under my belt the war was wearing on me—physically, spiritually, and emotionally. This experience seemed symbolic of everything I was feeling at the time.

NOTE

1. For a full description of each crew member's assignment, please refer to the Appendix.

CHAPTER 3

A Miracle Mission

By now the routine of the missions was nothing more than drudgery to be endured. When our crew name showed up on the flight list, we endured a sleepless night. At 0500 a flashlight would shine in our face and we'd crawl out of bed, get dressed, and go for breakfast. I found it odd that on some of these mornings I was famished, while on others I had no appetite at all. We always hoped for a "milk run" mission over a lightly defended target where we could go in, drop our bombs, and get out of there without having to face the black flak clouds that typified the defense of a more important military target. Unfortunately, such dream missions were few and far between.

It was about this time that we went on the second-most memorable mission of my military career. It was a raid on the Ploesti, Rumania Oil Refineries, the most heavily defended target in the Third Reich. Shortly after takeoff Jack Cook, our tail gunner, asked me to say a prayer for the crew, which I did over the interphone. When we were within range of the objective I looked out of the top gun turret. My gaze met an unbroken blanket of black smoke. The Nazis were already putting flak in our path, somehow guessing our course and altitude before we even got there. By the time we started to descend to the target the flak was unbelievable, literally shredding the metal skin of our aircraft until it looked like we were flying inside a giant sieve. As the aircraft reached a position called the Initial Point of Contact, the bombardier actually assumed control of the aircraft so he could maintain course and bearing until the moment the bombs were released. He did this using a sophisticated instrument called a Norden Bombsite, which allowed him to pilot the aircraft and release the bombs at the precise moment required to hit the target. To help everyone prepare for the inevitable jump in altitude that occurred when thousands of pounds of bombs were released, the bombardier always called out a ten-second countdown through the interphone. My heart raced at this moment, since we were most vulnerable while maintaining the constant speed and altitude needed to make an accurate drop. On this particular occasion Batch started his countdown, released the bombs, and the pilot resumed control and started a sharp banking maneuver to draw us away from the heaviest Triple A. Just then I felt the deep concussion of a flak explosion, and the aircraft lurched underneath my feet. From my position in the top turret I could see that the number-three engine had been hit. The copilot immediately feathered the prop, (moved the disabled propeller to a neutral position where it didn't interfere with the aerodynamics of the aircraft) and I shut down fuel lines to that engine to stave off a fire. The pilot dropped our altitude in response to the loss of power, and we started to limp back towards the safety of our own lines. The pilot instructed me to secure a damage control assessment from each member of the crew, and to report back on any damage. After all stations reported in, I was relieved to find that while we were peppered with holes, there were no injuries. The actual reporting went something like this.

Tail gunner, "We have quite a breeze back here from several large holes in the tail."

Waist gunners, "Ten to twelve obvious holes in the fuselage."

Lower ball turret gunner, "Visual inspection shows two or three large holes visible from this position."

Radio operator, "No damage visible, radio functional."

Navigator and Bombardier, "Two holes in the nose, but we have them plugged."

As Engineer, I completed a visual inspection from the upper turret, particularly searching for damage to the tail and engine cowls. I reported, "No obvious damage, except to the number three engine."

All in all, it was pretty bad, but the B-17 was still airworthy with three engines and adequate fuel. The fortunate thing about the B-17 was that it could take more of a beating than this and keep on going.

Our greatest danger at this point was from enemy fighters, particularly since we were flying alone. It was unsettling to watch all the other aircraft of the squadron disappear over the horizon on their way back to our home base in Italy. With three engines we couldn't maintain the required airspeed and altitude to stay with the squadron, and it would have placed all of them in danger to slow down for us.

We flew along for a while and saw nothing. Then the tail gunner reported that he saw several Messerschmitt ME109 and Focke-Wulf FW 190s coming at us from the aft position. Almost immediately we heard the rapid fire of the tail gunner's weapon. The enemy aircraft made several passes, firing away at us, when I suddenly heard the tail gunner scream through the interphone, "I'm hit Joe, please help me!" I disconnected from the main oxygen hose, put on the portable oxygen mask, and left my post to rush to his assistance. He was hit in the leg, and bleeding quite badly. I pulled him out of the tail position (a feat in itself since it was excruciating for him to straighten his leg from the kneeling position required in the tail) and dragged him to the radio room. I broke open the first-aid kid, cleaned the wound as best I could, put sulfur on it, then bandaged it to stop the bleeding. He wanted to go back to his position, but his leg was too injured to kneel on, so he had to stay where he was. Every so often the waist gunners and I would take turns going back to the tail to fire off a burst of rounds to make the enemy think this position was still manned. If they figured out that we were unarmed at that spot they would have focused their attack on that vulnerability. After moving the gun around, we rushed back to our own positions and fired from there.

The lower ball turret gunner, Shorty, cried out that he had been hit and his turret would not function. I had to manually crank him up and open the door without the benefit of the electric motors to get him out (for a full description of the positions, please refer to the Appendix). Shorty had been shot in the hand, and his fingers were badly mangled. I put him in the radio room and attended to his injured hand. By this time the aircraft had so many flak holes in it I had to watch where I was stepping to avoid tearing my flight suit on the razor sharp edges of the holes. Some holes were large enough that I could have fallen out of the aircraft.

The attack continued unabated, with the enemy fighters circling us like angry hornets attacking their victim. The adrenaline rush made us fight with everything we had to kill them before they killed us. They could smell blood and were anxious to add another flying fortress to their list of conquests. Just when I thought things couldn't get any worse, both the waist gunners were hit with disabling wounds. I dragged them to the radio room only to discover we had run out of bandages. The only thing I could think of was to shred a parachute and turn it into bandages. They protested that we might need the parachutes, but I had to do something to stop the bleeding.

Next, the bombardier was hit by shrapnel, which tore a large gash on the side of his head. He screamed for help in his microphone, and the navigator brought him back to the radio room where I was just finishing up with the waist gunners. I tore some more fabric from the parachute and wrapped it around the wounded area of his head. A red spot appeared in the fabric, but as I tightened it a bit more the bleeding stopped. I laid his head gently back to the floor, resting it on a parachute.

No sooner had the navigator returned to his position than I heard the explosion of a rocket blowing up near the nose of the aircraft. I crawled forward and found the navigator sprawled in a pool of blood, his body battered by the wind that was coming through a large, gaping hole in the Plexiglas nose of the aircraft. I recoiled at the sight, but fought back my fear and pulled him to the radio room to administer first aid.

Realizing that we had no defense against a forward assault, the radio operator moved to the navigator's position to fire the cheek guns. It wasn't long until he was hit in the chest. He somehow managed to cry for help into the interphone, and I moved forward to carry him back with the others. By now I was covered in blood and desperate to somehow help everybody survive.

Oh, the scene in that radio room—blood puddled on the floor, men writhing in agony from their wounds, and everyone terrified by the knowledge that we were completely defenseless. There were only three of us who remained uninjured (the pilot, copilot, and me). None of our machine guns were manned. Our aircraft was being buffeted by the air currents created by massive holes in all sections of the fuselage. A knockout blow could come at any moment, and we couldn't bail out because I had used the parachutes for bandages.

Just then the copilot called to me and said that Tonk, the pilot, had taken some shrapnel in the buttocks and I had to get him out of there fast. It was difficult to extract him from the seat, but we finally succeeded in getting him to the radio room to join the others. He was able to help me get the bleeding stopped, but he was in too much pain to assist in operating the aircraft.

I then stuck my head in the cockpit to see how our copilot, LoPriesti, was doing. He ordered me to climb into the pilot's seat, as the aircraft was very difficult to control and he needed my help. I took the seat and just then Batch, the bombardier, called and said, "Joe, if there is a God—and you claim there is one—would you please pray to him right now, and ask him to get us back to Italy safely?" Everyone joined in this call, so I prayed out loud through the interphone. It seemed to calm everyone down. After my prayer LoPriesti exclaimed, "Oh, my gosh! Look at what's headed our way, Joe!" I looked out the window to the 11:00 position and saw that the sky was full of fighter aircraft. It looked like a black cloud swarming towards us. We agreed that we were through and that we had better start looking for a place to crash land. Just then I glanced back out again and saw that the black cloud was our own P-38 fighters coming to protect us and drive off the enemy. As we told the rest of the crew, Batch said, "Maybe your God did hear us, Joe; we better talk more about it when we land." The radio operator remained at his station in spite of his wound, trying to establish contact with the fighters, but to no avail. His radio had obviously been disabled. At this point we were flying blind. Our compass and other navigational equipment was shot out and we had no way to find our way back to base. In the intensity of the battle we'd lost the number two engine, so we were now flying on just two engines, making it difficult to maintain altitude and the minimum airspeed required for flight. With no way to communicate with the fighter pilots to help us find our way home, it looked like a crash landing was inevitable in spite of their arrival. Just then one of the P38s broke out of formation and flew up next to us so close that I could see the pilot's face. He waved ahead to indicate we should follow him back to base. The rest of the P38s fanned out to protect us from the German fighters. It looked like we might have a chance of getting back to safety after all. I was so grateful for these pilots that I said a loud thank-you to God. We followed the fighter pilot's lead for some time until we could see the blue waters of the Adriatic Sea out of the front windows, and what a glorious sight it was. In just a few moments the runway came into view, and I could see ambulances and fire trucks waiting.

At this point it took all the skill our copilot possessed to prepare the aircraft for landing. Many of our controls had been shot up so badly that it took our combined strength to hold the aircraft in proper position. As we made a banking turn into our final approach the number four engine went out, and I looked down to see that we had only about twenty-five gallons of aviation fuel left for the sole remaining engine. We'd burn through that in just a few moments, leaving us with no power to stabilize the aircraft during landing or to operate the hydraulic systems needed to deploy the landing gear. As I reached to put the landing gear down I could tell that the aircraft was losing altitude fast. I only hoped that it locked into position. The cockpit instruments were nonfunctional, so the copilot had to make a "seat of the pants" landing, relying only on his experience and feel for the aircraft. This was an amazing challenge with three engines out, since the natural reaction of the aircraft was to turn in the opposite direction of the engine that is providing thrust. Our copilot had to fight this tendency by holding the rudder in an opposing position to keep the aircraft on a proper approach. Call it the grace of God, but we actually made a good, solid landing. As the wheels touched the ground I heard the guys in the radio room let out a cheer and break into relieved laughter. We both "stood on the brakes" the moment we had firm contact with the ground.

Just when it looked like we'd make a clean landing, another problem came into view. About midway down the runway an Italian worker was using a steamroller to work on the surface. I could see the panic in his face when he saw our unexpected approach, and I prayed that he'd clear the runway before we got there. To my horror he jumped off and started running, leaving the steamroller in our path. The last thing I remember seeing was the steamroller pass under the right wing of the aircraft. Everything went black as I was knocked unconscious.

When I came to I was disoriented and couldn't figure out where I was. As my mind cleared, I realized that I was in the nose of the aircraft with the Norden Bombsight wrapped around my neck. I was upside down, with dirt in my throat and face. I then heard someone say, "He must be in there, but he can't be alive." Then another voice said, "Too bad, he's the only one left!" I was too disoriented to say anything. I didn't know if I was alive or if I was dreaming. Finally I got my wits about me enough to cry out "I'm in here, please help me get out!" I heard startled voices say, "He's alive! It's a miracle!" and "Be careful, but let's hurry." They cut me out of the mangled cockpit and helped me to my feet. My ankle hurt and I could feel a cut on the top of my head. Painfully, I started to walk. The mechanics who cut me out of the aircraft tried to help, but I told them I was okay and asked about the rest of the crew. They said they were all on their way to the hospital.

Two debriefing officers came to take me away, but I paused to stop and look back at the aircraft. I couldn't believe what I saw. Apparently we had hit the steamroller with the tail section of the aircraft. Since it had so many holes from enemy fire, that section had torn off from the main fuselage, causing the front end of the aircraft to take a nosedive into the dirt. The nose of the aircraft hit with such force that it peeled the fuselage open like a banana, and threw me through the instrument panel and into the nose of the aircraft. Damage crews were taking pictures of the wreckage with astonished looks in their eyes. One of the doctors had returned by this point, and he wanted me to go directly to the hospital by ambulance. I probably should have gone, but I declined, saying I was okay. He looked me over and patched up my head, then helped me get in the car that would take me to head-quarters for a debriefing. The debriefing officers offered me a drink and I gratefully accepted a glass of Coke. They started asking a long list of questions that included when and where we got hit, what kind of fighters attacked, and how many men were wounded. They also asked me what I was doing in the pilot's seat. As I answered their questions, a scribe who was taking notes said under his breath, "This is incredible! You'll be put in for the Distinguished Flying Cross for sure." Though this award was a rare honor given to those who showed "extraordinary achievement" in air combat, I hadn't really had time to think about that, and right then I didn't care.

As I recounted the story, I was amazed to think about everything that had happened and how I'd somehow had the presence of mind to care for all those wounded men. It struck me as interesting that my first assignment in the army was to train as a medic, which I thought to be a huge mistake at the time. I'd been relieved to transfer into the air corps. Yet even though my time in the medical corps was brief, the instruction and practice I gained undoubtedly helped me handle the urgent needs that developed on this flight. I was also grateful that we had landed behind Allied, rather than enemy, lines.

After what seemed an hour or two of questioning, (though I'm sure it was much less) I started trembling from shock. They helped me into a Jeep and transported me to our tent. I went in and flopped down on my cot to try to calm down, but my mind replayed the events of the flight over and over again. I found myself particularly focusing on the huge holes in the aircraft, and the miracle of landing with just one engine and twenty-five gallons of fuel. If the runway had been just two minutes further away, we'd have been helpless. We were so blessed to have all ten of us make it back alive. As the only one who hadn't been taken straight to the hospital, I couldn't help but ask the question, "Why me, why was I spared?" There was no answer, but I did feel with all my heart that God was protecting me for other experiences, even though I had no idea what they would be.

I was so overwhelmed with emotion and gratitude that I bore my testimony to God that I knew He lived and that I knew He heard and answered our prayers. Suddenly I felt His spirit come over me as I never had before, and I wanted to shout from the rooftops that God is real and He will listen to those who call on Him. Forgotten were the depths of great darkness I had felt in my soul from the chilling events my crew-mates and I had passed through. I now felt my spirit illuminated by the light of His spirit. I knew that as long as I lived, I would never forget that moment. No matter what adverse circumstances I found myself in again, I could count on God to help me according to His will.

I cleaned up and after a long, hot shower, I returned to the empty tent. As I sat on the edge of my cot, I broke down and started sobbing. All the emotions I had suppressed during the mission now over-whelmed me. I later thought about writing it all down in a letter to Afton, but I just couldn't see how I could share this experience with her, at least not at this time. It was too unbelievable and disturbing. While it might have helped me to talk about it, I could just imagine her reading and fretting about the letter on the other side of the world. I had to keep this experience to myself. I couldn't even talk it over with my buddies, since they were in the hospital. Even though there were thousands of men on the base, I was lonesome for my crew, and I was so relieved when some of the men with less serious wounds came back to the tent a few days later. As I visited with the crew I found out that they all believed in "my" God now, and they thanked me for turning to Him for help during the flight. Apparently, adversity ignites the fires of faith in even the most ardent unbelievers. I was grateful to talk with them and know that they would be okay.

I didn't receive any orders for the next few days, which was a blessing on one hand and a curse on the other. I don't think I could have gone back to regular duties with all the shaking and trembling I was experiencing. On the other hand, just lying around the base with nothing to do allowed too much time for my thoughts to run away. I was relieved when new orders came telling me that I was to be given ten days of "R & R" (rest and relaxation) on the Isle of Capri, thirty minutes by boat off the coast of Italy in the most scenic part of the Mediterranean. Fortunately, two of my buddies were far enough along in their recovery to join me. When we arrived on the beautiful little island we were taken to a hotel where I was given a private room with a bed and pillow. It felt luxurious to have clean sheets and pillowcases. I hadn't felt anything like it since engineering school nearly two years earlier. I could sleep in as late as I wanted, and then go downstairs to breakfast or order room service to the sunny little room they'd arranged for me. During the day I loved walking around the village and chatting with my buddies or other soldiers that we met. The fresh sea air, the sunny skies, and the absence of the smells and sounds of combat really did work to lift our morale. There was a pretty active nightlife, with open-air cafes serving wonderful food and beverages, and there was always music and dancing. The island was famous for its Italian wines, which my buddies relished. We could have anything we wanted at the army's expense. I liked sitting at a table listening to the music and the sound of people laughing. In some ways it reminded me of going out with my friends in Salt Lake City to a drive-in on State Street in the days before the war. My mind was pulling itself back together again, and it was good to relax.

The nights were still a challenge, though. On more than one occasion I found myself sitting up in bed screaming. In the only dream I remember, I shouted coordinates to the gunners as we came under an intense attack from enemy fighters. Then I heard sobbing, hysterical voices crying, "I've been hit Joe, help me, help me!" Then blood. I'd wake up in a sweat, my chest heaving in and out like I was in the middle of running a marathon. Thank heavens for the softness of the sheets and the smell of the ocean air through the open window to help me remember where I was. It helped me calm down and go to sleep again.

One of the most enjoyable experiences during our leave was the chance to take a rowboat out to the famous "Blue Grotto." The entrance to the cavern was underwater when the tide was in, so it took an experienced guide to enter at just the right time. Once inside, the light from outside turned the water aquamarine, and it reflected on the walls of the grotto in a thousand shifting patterns that made it feel like we'd entered an enchanted paradise. It was soothing to my spirit to sit in this quiet, secluded spot and to reflect on the beauty of God's creation. The world would have been perfect if only Afton could have been there to enjoy it with me.

When our leave was over and my buddies and I returned to Foggia, some of the officers called me into an interview to see how I was holding up. They told me that two members of our crew had been replaced because of their injuries. It was incredible that out of the ten of us that had trained together in Tennessee, seven were still members of the crew. Fortunately, the new guys were veterans that fit in easily. Soon we were operating at full efficiency.

As the squadron approached the target on our first combat mission after the crash, I found myself mentally picturing the dozens of aircraft starting to drop their payloads, filling the sky with hundreds of falling bombs that could easily destroy buildings, runways, ships, people, roadways, railroad trains, railroad tracks, trees, houses, flowers, museums, schools, factories, ammunition dumps (those were really impressive), oil refineries, gasoline storage tanks, families, trucks, cars, animals, gardens, barns . . . I was sick to my stomach thinking about the damage we were inflicting. I hadn't really thought much about it before, but after our near brush with death I couldn't help but think of the terrible toll the war was taking on all of us—friend and foe alike. I guess I hadn't healed as much emotionally as I thought I had.

CHAPTER 4

Blown From the Sky

It was getting close. The goal of fifty missions was now within reach, and we could no longer pretend not to be excited. Oh, everybody talked tough, and the airman's superstition kept us from saying too much to each other, but the end was in sight. I found myself fantasizing about what it would be like to have a stateside assignment. Maybe I would be an instructor back in California. That would be great since Afton and Randy could come and join me. Or I might be assigned to inspect and go on test flights of new aircraft rolling off the assembly lines. That would be okay too, since the Boeing factory was in Seattle, Washington, just a short flight from Salt Lake City. It didn't really matter, because one way or another I'd be safely back in the States and close to my family. I even wrote to Afton to tell her how excited everyone was getting.

We had a real scare on our 43rd mission, though. It was a raid on the Rumanian oil fields once again, which was the most dangerous assignment they could give. I had been there five times before and had seen so many aircraft shot down that I lost count. At any rate, we woke up at 0500 as usual, and went through our preflight drill. Takeoff was routine, and we soon reached the altitude where we could test our weapons. We were flying left wing on this particular mission. Suddenly the left waist gunner on the right wing aircraft started to test his weapon when it ran away from him. He momentarily lost control and the muzzle inclined up while he was firing. In short, he shot directly at us! Fortunately, he didn't hit anybody, although he scared the wits out of our radioman, who called to me for help. I did a visual inspection that revealed a number of holes in the fuselage.

That wasn't near as bad as the fact that he'd shot up three of our parachutes. I told the pilot that we were short three parachutes—a disaster waiting to happen on a Ploesti raid. He made the decision to abort the mission, so we peeled out of position and returned to base. There was a huge sigh of relief from everyone on board. Fortunately, they gave us credit for the mission since it was such a close call, and nobody argued. They could have scrubbed our last seven missions before reaching fifty, and it would have been okay with us.

That evening we could hear the aircraft returning, and we went out to count them coming in. Four didn't make it back, and one of the aircraft that did return had three dead crewmen on board. The entire camp was silent that night knowing that more of our friends would never again see their families.

The infantry had been moving rapidly through Italy, and we now thought we might have a chance to visit Rome on R & R after completing our fifty missions. That was pretty exciting to me since I had read so much about that great ancient city. I hoped that it hadn't been ruined too much by the war and that the Roman Coliseum and catacombs were still intact. I was told that there was a pretty good chance I would get to go, and this brightened my spirits.

The next five missions were completed without problem, in spite of a few harrowing moments. It grated on my nerves to think we were getting so close, and I prayed constantly that we'd make it back safely.

We were now down to just two missions before qualifying to go stateside, and the excitement of the crew was almost tangible. Still, I kept reminding myself that more than one crew had made it to mission forty-nine or fifty only to be shot down, so I had to keep my exuberance in check. As our 49th mission approached, I checked the board one day to discover that we were scheduled for the following morning. I went back to the tent and started packing everything that I didn't think I would need between the forty-ninth and fiftieth missions (like books and extra clothing). Then I dashed off a note to Afton telling her I'd be home almost as soon as the letter.

The next morning the whole crew was uptight as we went to our briefing. They uncovered a new map and announced that we'd be flying to Breslau, Germany. I had never heard of the town before, but I could see that it was way up north on the Polish border, so it would be a long flight. Our assigned altitude was higher than usual, which meant it would be difficult for their Triple A to hit us, but the flight was so long we would spend most of it out of the protective range of our fighters. They dismissed us with a cheerful "Good luck!" and my regular crew and I went to the waiting jeeps for transport to the flight line. We'd been hoping for a milk run, but we knew we weren't going to get it because of the length of time in the air over enemy territory without the protection of our own fighter aircraft. The greater the distance, the greater the exposure to enemy fire.

As part of our standard preparation for a mission we were issued maps of the area, emergency food rations, a pistol, compass, and instructions on what to do if we had to go down. Once airborne, we chatted a bit after reaching altitude, which was not a normal procedure. Someone would ask another crewmember what he planned to do when he got back to the States, and then it would go around the interphone until everyone had chimed in. We talked about our families and how much we missed them. The seven of us who had been together since training in Tennessee now had forty-eight missions together, and we knew just about everything about each other and our families. We also speculated about the three members of the original crew who had already departed, and we hoped we'd get a chance to see them someday. We had never talked like this before, and it felt good to pass the time this way.

On the way to the target we encountered some enemy fighters, but we fought them off just as we were coming near the objective. Everybody turned "all business" again. We resorted to our usual silence except for the formal reporting protocol, where each member of the crew periodically reported their status. There were instances on other aircraft in which an enemy bullet killed a member of the crew so quickly and silently that no one knew he was dead until later in the flight. Soon all thoughts focused in on the aircraft factory we'd been assigned to blow up. We were flying in the Tail End Charlie position.

When the pilot said, "Okay, we are turning on the Initial Point of Contact, Batch, it's all yours." I found myself praying, "Please hit the target the first time so we don't have to make another run at it." Batch took control of the aircraft, and then came on the interphone and started counting down from ten. When he reached five it was my responsibility to leave my position to go back and check that the bomb bay doors had opened properly. Just as I turned to leave my turret, I saw the lead aircraft take a direct hit to one of its engines. The loss of power caused the aircraft to immediately lose airspeed, and in something like a split second they were above us in the air, with their bomb bay doors wide open! It all happened so quickly that they unknowingly dropped all their bombs at once. I heard myself screaming, "Oh, my gosh . . . " I saw one of their bombs hit our right wing. Then it was black.

I don't know how long I was knocked unconscious, but when I came to it took me a few moments to figure out what was going on. Apparently our aircraft had been blown apart by the bombs of our lead aircraft. I found myself in a tubular section of the fuselage that was open on both ends, spinning in the air as we fell towards the ground four miles below. My aircraft had been so mangled that I couldn't even figure out what part of the airplane I was in, nor could I focus on other debris outside the section that held me because of the spinning motion. I always wore a parachute while over the target area, so I instinctively felt my chest to make sure it was there. A lot of airmen sat on their parachute during a long flight to provide some padding, since military aircraft weren't designed for comfort.

I was relieved to feel that my parachute was in place, but I couldn't use it because I was stuck against the wall of fuselage, held there by the centrifugal force. It was similar to a child spinning a bucket of water. No water would escape even when the bucket circled in an arc over the child's head. In this instance, I was like the water, and I couldn't get out. I'd try to get up only to be forced back against the wall. In desperation I looked down and saw one of my crewmates lying next to me. I reached out and touched him, but he didn't move. Apparently the explosion had killed him. I knew that I had to muster every ounce of energy I had or I would go down to my death in that section of the aircraft. I tried several times, but to no avail. I was just too weak to pull free, and so the only thing I could do was pray. I asked the Lord to please help me get out somehow. I said it out loud, the words choking in my throat, but He heard me anyway.

Suddenly, as clear and as calm as if she was standing right next to me in the living room of our home, I heard the voice of my wife Afton say, "Joe, look down at your legs and you'll see that there's a cable holding them. Pull the cable!" That's all she said. I looked around, but couldn't see anyone. Even though I was stunned, I looked down and sure enough there was a cable lying across my legs. I reached down and pulled it with all my might. At first nothing happened, but then I was suddenly sucked out of the fuselage and started freefalling. I later learned that the cable was attached to two pins that held an escape hatch door. When I pulled them loose, the door separated from the fuselage. Talk about incredible. It probably took a second or two for me to get over the shock of being hit by the wind, but then I realized that I was falling backwards through space. I can actually remember talking to myself and saying, "Joe, you're falling to the ground—do something!" I reached forward and grabbed the handle of the rip cord on my chest parachute, giving it a firm tug. Nothing happened. I jerked it as hard as I could. Suddenly it broke free in my hand, and I thought to myself, "You just broke your parachute!" Next, I was startled by a loud pop, and an instant later I felt the straps under my legs tighten up. It was like I was standing still in mid-air. I looked up to see my chute fully open above me. It was the first time I had ever parachuted out of an aircraft, and there I was drifting down into enemy territory, far behind their lines.

About this time I looked forward and saw a man who was falling right in front of me. I could see that his chute was out of the pack, but it hadn't opened up at the top. He was frantically trying to pull on the cables to get the chute to open. I looked at his face and recognized that it was our pilot, Ron Tonkovich. There was nothing I could do, and I had to watch him fall to the ground at full speed. I was sickened by the sight of him hitting the ground with such force that the impact created a big crater. One of my best friends had just died right before my eyes, and my mind had trouble understanding what was happening. I said a prayer of thanks that my chute had opened, and I thanked God for bringing me the miracle of hearing Afton's voice to help me out. It was almost surreal, like everything was happening faster than I could comprehend, yet almost like it was in slow motion. I looked up at my chute to discover that it was extended out almost parallel with me because of the strong breeze. I was swishing back and forth, back and forth, in the wind.

As I looked down at the ground I could see that there were both soldiers and civilians waiting for me to land—their rifles pointed at me. I thought I could faintly hear the sound of rifle fire from their direction. The Lord preserved my life again by prompting me to reach down in my pant leg and throw out my pistol. If I had landed with small arms on me they would have treated me like a paratrooper and shot me on sight. I kept my maps and C rations for food. At that moment my mind was spinning, and thoughts were flooding through my consciousness too fast for me to concentrate. Yet somehow it seemed like eternity passed as I drifted down through the white clouds, and I was surprised that there was almost no sensation of movement. It was as if the ground were coming up to meet me instead of me falling down to it. I had no choice but to remain as calm as I could on the outside, while inwardly hoping they wouldn't shoot me. As I drifted lazily towards the ground, it struck me that this was Randy's first birthday—and to think that his dad was in such a predicament. It was Friday, September 13, 1944.

I kept looking up and around to see if there were any other parachutes, but the sky was empty. As I got closer, I could see that the civilians had bats, clubs, shovels, and pitchforks, and it looked like they wanted to beat me to death with them. I just kept praying silently for help, and I desperately hoped that somehow I'd survive.

All of a sudden my lazy descent turned into a rush as the distance to the ground narrowed. I hit much harder than I expected, with about the same force as you'd feel jumping off the roof of a tall house. I had been taught to bend my knees and relax when I hit, and to then roll to absorb the shock, but my mind was racing too much to remember any of that at the time. So, I hit the ground like a sack of potatoes thrown off a moving truck, and it knocked the wind out of me.

As I struggled to get up, the civilians pointed and gestured to where my pilot had landed. They laughed at the look on my face. Then they came at me with their pitchforks, shovels, and clubs. One woman hit me with a club and I stumbled to the ground. I said to myself, "Joe, bite your lip and say to yourself 'they can't hurt me.'" I rolled up like a ball and waited for the next blow. They were all screaming at me in angry, hateful voices, but I didn't understand a word. Finally, two guards came up and prodded me with their bayonets while shouting "Geh raus!" When I didn't respond instantly, they stuck their bayonets in me hard enough to penetrate my flight suit and tear the skin. I struggled to my feet. They motioned for me to pick up the parachute, which was a heavy jumble of fabric and lines. As I was picking it up one of the soldiers slammed me with the butt of his weapon and yelled at me, while pointing the direction he wanted me to go. I stumbled forward as best I could, but the cords of the parachute trailed behind me in such a way that the guards could stomp on them, which would swing me around or drag me to the ground. They found it quite funny. To keep the show going they'd hit me with their guns until I staggered up and started moving again. I tried to wind the cords around my arms to take up the slack, but whenever I started to make progress they'd just stomp on them again and prod me with their bayonets. It made me angry, of course, but I reminded myself that I had to take it or they might just pull the trigger or stab me. After all, who else was there to protect me? If anyone ever asked what happened, they could always claim that I was trying to escape and so they had to shoot me. I swallowed my anger and kept trudging along as best I could. Even though they were bullying me and antagonizing me any way they could, it was fortunate that the soldiers got to me when they did. I believe the civilians would have killed me if they hadn't been restrained. All the time we were marching, the civilians followed along hollering and spitting at me, and I could see that they wanted to get at me with their shovels and pitchforks. I had to dodge them or run the risk of getting smacked by a shovel—or worse.

It was about 1600 in the afternoon (4:00 P.M.) and it was already getting pretty cold. I'm sure I felt the cold more acutely than the locals since I had been living in the hot to temperate areas of Africa and Italy. At these northern latitudes the sky was already starting to darken into dusk. When it seemed like I had walked for a mile or so my legs became so shaky that I felt like I couldn't go much farther without a rest. I paused for a moment and both guards pounced on me with a fury that sent me to the ground. I forced myself to stand and start moving forward again. Fortunately, at this point the soldiers pushed me towards a building ahead. As I went through the doors the civilians inside strained to get a look at me, and many shouted heated remarks that were probably insults. I had bombed their homes and factories, killing both civilians and soldiers, and now I was in their domain. The guards searched me and took everything I had in my pockets. Then they threw me down a flight of stairs and shoved me through a door into a cement cell that had no windows. I fell forward and sprawled on the floor, face first. I heard the door slam shut, and then listened as a heavy bolt slid into place, locking me in. For the first time in my life I had lost my freedom, and my stomach ached with the anxiety this created.

I lay there for a few moments and then rolled over to take a look around. The room was unpainted and bleak. A small light bulb was hanging from the ceiling, probably about 40 watts, but it was so high up that I couldn't see it clearly. There was also a small table and wooden chair. I was really cold now that I had stopped moving, but there were no blankets or heating devices, so I sat on the floor shivering. It's amazing how fast a cold cement floor can sap the warmth from your body. I was very hungry, and I hurt all over from my rough parachute landing and the kicks and hits I had endured on the march. I wanted to cry, but I reminded myself that I had to be tough and not let the Germans know how desperate I felt. As I calmed down I noticed that I had a small shrapnel wound on my wrist. The blood had dried so that it posed no danger, but it still hurt. I sat there shaking and thinking a million thoughts about Afton and my crew, and I wondered helplessly if I would ever see my family again. I hoped some of my crew had made it out, but I hadn't seen any parachutes so I feared the worst. My world was pretty bleak that cold autumn night in a hostile little corner of Germany, and I felt lonesome and forlorn. All I could do was sit and wonder what was coming next.

CHAPTER 5

From the Frying Pan to the Fire

I don't know how long I sat in the cell. It's hard to measure time when there are no external indications like light or darkness. I was desperately tired, but so many thoughts crowded into my mind that it was impossible to sleep. My mind drifted back across the events of the day, and I remembered our cheerful conversations through the interphone. My crewmates were like brothers, and as far as I knew, they had all been killed—by our own bombs, no less. It was unbelievable. One moment we were planning what to do when we got home, and now, just hours later, I was all alone in a cement room deep behind enemy lines, without anyone to talk to or to share in the pain I felt. I'm sure I was scared, but the predominant emotion was the sorrow I felt over losing my friends, and my heart ached more than my injured limbs. I hoped that somehow, at least some of them had made it out alive and that I just hadn't seen their parachutes. I tried to convince myself to quit thinking about the terror I felt when I regained consciousness only to find our aircraft destroyed, yet my mind reviewed it again and again. To comfort myself and to suppress the panic, I thought about each of the men I had served with since Tennessee.

Ron Tonkovich had proven himself a superb aircraft commander. His quiet, unassuming style was very different from the devil-may-care attitude you saw in fighter pilots, but it was perfect for managing a crew of ten people. When someone got hurt or excited, Ron's voice would come on the interphone to give an order in a way that seemed to soothe everyone's shaken nerves. I never once saw him panic, no matter how bad the flak or enemy aircraft fire was. When he got hit on the mission to Ploesti he didn't shout or curse, he just said he was hit and thanked me for helping him out of his seat. I knew he was in intense pain, but he didn't complain at all. One of the memories of Ron that helped me smile was recalling going to the beach with him and watching how much fun he had swimming. The vision of Ron falling to the earth while struggling to get his parachute open intruded on these pleasant thoughts, and I mourned for his fiancée and for Ron's family.

Because Dick LoPriesti was so gregarious and outgoing, it was almost impossible to get angry with him, even when his nervous energy put everyone else on edge. He'd get pretty excited when enemy fire shot up our aircraft, but always stayed at his station to help Ron control the aircraft. I gained incredible respect for Dick when he landed the aircraft after three engines had failed. This was a feat that took remarkable skill and concentration, but he pulled it off perfectly.

"Batch," the bombardier, was the person who had given me the most trouble, but I think I may have missed him the most. He always acted so tough in his insistence that there was no God and that only the emotionally weak-minded needed to rely on the belief in an outside being for support and comfort, but inside I think he wanted to believe. One of Batch's favorite sayings was "Nothing happens by design, it just happens!" He'd bring that up whenever I was having a religious discussion with one of the other men. On one occasion I'd had enough of his teasing, so another crew member and I set him up for a practical joke. We found some piano wire and strung it about three inches above the ground between two stakes in front of Batch's tent. When the siren for dinner sounded Batch bounded out of the tent at full-speed only to trip on the wire. He fell face first into the dust. Old Batch jumped up hopping mad, shouting "Who did that, who strung that wire?" Trying to suppress our grins, we said, "Why Batch, nothing happens by design, it just happens." Boy was he mad. I thought he might chase us down and beat us, which would have been pretty easy since we were laughing so hard. But then he got the joke and started laughing with us. After that he didn't give me so much trouble. I think his faith in "no-faith" was shaken on our miracle mission when so many small miracles happened to save our lives. I hoped now that our occasional conversations about God might be helping him as he crossed the veil to the spirit world—if he had indeed died in the explosion that destroyed our aircraft. There was one thing about my religious beliefs that Batch did like, namely, the fact that my convictions prevented me from drinking alcohol. After a mission, each of us were entitled to a free shot of whiskey. I'd always pass mine to someone else on the crew. On more than one occasion Batch would come up and put his arm around me and say, "Hey buddy, you could do me a real favor if you let me have your shot of whiskey today!" He knew full well that everybody got a turn—he just liked to tease me.

Our navigator had been the most excited to reach the fiftieth mission so he could return to the United States. He was extremely capable at his assigned duties, and could calculate our position in the most trying of circumstances when called on by the pilot. He didn't like sitting up in the nose of the aircraft where he could see the flak or enemy fighter cover that we were about to fly into. He'd usually say something like, "Uh-oh, here it comes, I'm going to come back and trade places with one of you guys—who's it going to be?" Yet he never left his station.

Tom Hynes, one of our original waist gunners, had an arm severely wounded on a previous mission, and had been sent home early. Before he left he asked me to pray with him privately, particularly when it looked like he would be permanently disabled by his injury. I told him I'd like to teach him to pray, but he was uncomfortable with that, so I prayed that his arm might be healed. We received a letter from Tom just a few weeks before our final mission telling us that much to the surprise of his doctors he'd responded unusually well to physical therapy, and had regained almost the full use of his arm. He was sure that he could return to his craft as a precision welder to support his family. I felt that his recovery was a direct answer to our prayers.

Mike, our other waist gunner, had been one of my best friends, perhaps because we shared a love of the aircraft and its mechanical systems. He almost always helped me with the aircraft inspections, and we sometimes traded positions so he could act in the role of flight engineer.

The other two faces that came to mind were those of our tail gunner, Jack Cook, who had suffered so much when he was shot up on the miracle mission, and Shorty Krasnouskie, our lower ball turret gunner. I always wondered how Shorty could stand it down in the ball turret without getting claustrophobic. He literally had to lay with the controls of the turret and machine gun between his legs. His range of vision above him was obscured by the body of the aircraft, yet he could see thousands of feet below to the ground when looking through the opening below his feet. It took immense courage for him to go into the turret on each of the missions. I always felt a kind of kinship with Shorty since he was morally straight and inspired by beautiful music and art. While that wasn't exactly the same as the religious conviction that sustained me, it showed that he respected the finer things in life, and revealed him to be a refined and gentle person.

I realized how much each of these men meant to me, and I grieved at the thought of their death.

Perhaps an hour or two after being locked up I was startled to hear the sharp noise of the rusty bolt being opened on the door. Two rough-looking guards with weapons pointed at me shouted, "Geh raus," and I struggled to my feet and moved past them out the door. Apparently I wasn't moving fast enough, so they kicked me up the stairs and prodded me with the muzzles of their rifles. I found myself hoping that their rough handling wouldn't "accidentally" discharge the weapons. When we reached the end of a long hallway, I was ushered into a large interrogation room. An immaculately groomed German officer sat behind a large wooden desk. He didn't look up as I entered. A guard shouted at me in German, apparently telling me to sit down in the solitary chair in front of the desk, but I didn't understand. He shoved me into the chair with such force that I had to hold on or I would have toppled to the ground. I kept my eyes down, waiting for their next move, glancing up only occasionally to see the officer just staring at me. After a long pause he said in perfect English, "So, sergeant, what is your name and where do you come from?" I was so startled to hear English again that I almost answered his question. The truth was, I wanted desperately to talk to someone—anyone—and tell them what had happened to me that day. For just a moment I wanted to pour my heart out to this man, and I could have very easily started sobbing. But after a short pause to collect my thoughts, my military training took over and I remembered proper protocol. I replied that my name was Joseph Banks, Rank of Staff Sergeant, Serial Number 39910833. He wrote that down patiently and then asked me again, "So, Sergeant Banks, what base do you fly out of and what was your intended objective today?"

When I didn't reply he went on, "By the way, what kind of aircraft did you serve in, and what happened to your crewmates? Did any of them make it out?" Up to this point he had been very polite and almost friendly, as if he wanted to help me out. I followed proper procedure and reported the same information again: name, rank, and serial number. This really annoyed him, and suddenly his cool demeanor darkened. He turned to me with an angry glare and said, "You will cooperate with us sergeant, or you will be very, very sorry!" I silently stared back at him. He ordered the guard to take me back to my room to think things over for a while. Back I went to my tiny cell, with a gun in my back the whole way. Then came the dreadful sound of the bolt being locked in place. I didn't know what time it was since they'd confiscated my watch, but I did know that I was very hungry, cold, and terrified about my future.

After a few moments alone I took some deep breaths to calm down, then laid my head on the table and closed my eyes to see if I could sleep. There were so many thoughts racing through my mind that it didn't seem like I fell asleep, yet I was startled awake sometime later when the door slammed open. The guard took me back to the same interrogation room. This time the officer got up and walked around a bit before asking questions. He asked how big a bomb load we carried, how our aircraft was destroyed, and what gave us the right to drop bombs on women and children. Some of his questions were designed to disarm me, others to goad me. It was one thing to be told in a classroom in Tennessee that all you had to do was give name, rank, and serial number, and quite another to be seated in front of a German officer deep inside enemy territory, with an armed guard pointing his weapon at your head. I said a mental prayer and felt that I was doing okay, so I just responded as before. The officer looked at me quizzically, as if he were pondering why I would be this foolish, and then he offered me a cigarette. In those days, cigarettes were the universal medium of exchange and a highly desirable commodity. When I refused his offer he violently slammed the lid of his cigarette case and swore at me in words that were perfectly understandable and offensive.

He signaled to the guards for what they'd been waiting for. I grimaced as they used the butt of their guns to knock me off my chair, and then they kicked me in the ribs with steel-toed boots. The pain was unbelievably sharp and my body recoiled from the blows. I wanted to cry out, but I managed to stifle my response into a grunting sound that made them laugh and kick me again. I'd have given anything to holler or scream, but I bit my lip until it bled, which helped me suppress the natural reaction to cry out. When they'd had their fun, they hit me one more time and then told me to pick up the chair and sit in it. The officer asked me the questions again, but I only gave him a weak "name, rank, and serial number."

He smiled at this and told me that I would be even more sorry than I could possibly imagine. He then beckoned to the door and said something to the guards in German. They shoved me out into the hallway for another trip back to my cell. Apparently he had instructed them to trip me at the top of the stairs, because just as I was looking down to get my footing a guard punched me in the back hard enough to knock me off balance. I tumbled down the cement stairs, landing in a heap at the bottom. I was so exhausted and hurt that I wanted to just lay there, but the guards started kicking me until I half-crawled, half-ran into my cell. They gave me a final kick through the open door. Before they could shut the door, I pleaded with one of the guards for permission to go to the bathroom. He just slammed the door in my face. I lay on the floor for a long time, trying to catch my breath. The urge to go to the bathroom plagued me, and I held on as long as I could until I finally thought I would explode. I started pounding on the door for the guard. After a lot of shouting I was taken by the guard to a room that smelled like a bathroom but didn't have any fixtures. He pointed to a cement wall with a small trough at the bottom where the prisoners would urinate and gravity would slowly drain it through a hole in the wall. No flushing or water to wash it down. The guard watched me while I went, and as soon as I started to button my trousers he jabbed me in the back with his rifle and marched me back to my room at double time. I clutched my pants all the way to keep them from falling down.

As cold and as harsh as it was, I was grateful to be alone again. I sat in the chair, put my head down in my arms, and said a prayer of gratitude that the Lord had helped my chute to open and that I had heard Afton's voice to help me get out of the aircraft. I was frightened about what would happen, but at least I was alive. My thoughts again returned to the horrifying sight of seeing Ron Tonkovich fall past me. As my mind replayed the sight of his awful, frantic plunge to death, I wept. I prayed that he was warm and safe now in the spirit world. It was like losing a big brother—the guy who was always in control and always calm in a crisis. Now I was in the worst crisis of my life and I was all alone. I was sick from what I had been through, and even more sick wondering what had happened to all my buddies. I was so tired by this point that I cradled my head in my arms, hoping that I could go to sleep and wake up to find that it was all just a really bad dream.

Time passed—I don't know how long—but it seemed like three or four days. Finally they brought me some water and some dark, heavy bread with sawdust in it. It didn't matter to me. It was like being served a Thanksgiving Day feast, and I savored the taste of food in my mouth and the feeling of having something in my stomach. I was very weak by this point and even a little food gave instant relief from the pain in my stomach.

A few hours later they ordered me upstairs to meet the English-speaking officer again. This time he got right to business, with no cheerful or kind tones in his voice. He told me that I was Joe Banks from Salt Lake City, Utah, and that I was married to Afton Banks and we had an infant son. He then told me in no uncertain terms that if I didn't cooperate with every question he asked me, my family could be hurt. So what was it going to be? Would I give them the information they wanted, or would I make it tough on myself and my family? A wave of despair and terror swept over me. How could they possibly know about my family? Someone must have had connections in Salt Lake City, which meant they really could pose a threat to the people I loved. I felt that I still had the strength and determination to take whatever they gave me, but what about Afton? My tortured thoughts were interrupted by his harsh demand, "Well, what's it going to be, Banks?" I said a desperate silent prayer asking what I should do.

A distinct impression came to my mind that I should hold the line, so I said as firmly as my voice would let me, "My name is Joseph Banks, Staff Sergeant, Serial Number 39910833." The officer let out a nearly inhuman growl and turned the guards loose on me. They attacked ferociously, like dogs attacking a rabbit, and their blows and kicks forced me to the ground in agony. When I pulled myself up off the floor the officer said I was in deep trouble, so I had better think care-fully about what I was going to do. He said he would talk to me again soon. The thought that kept racing through my mind was "How does he know about Afton and Randy and where we live?" It made me frantic to think they might be watching them at this very moment. My mind reasoned that it was impossible for there to be German spies in far-off Utah, so I figured they must have access to some kind of civil records or something. Still, he sounded so confident about how they could hurt us that I couldn't help but have doubts about my family's safety.

It was at least another day before I was called back, since they brought me a slice of black bread and water in the meantime. The dreadful moment came when I once again stumbled up the stairs and into the interrogation room. When my friends back in high school had nicknamed me "Tough" they had no idea how severely that name would be tested. But there had to be some truth to it because I was getting pretty stubborn by now. I didn't think I could ever hate anyone, but the beatings inflicted by the German interrogators were inhuman. My anger and indignation mixed with fear to give me some kind of emotional reserve to draw on. I knew that *this* interrogation was probably going to be worse than any previous ones.

The interesting thing was that I don't think I had any information that would have helped them, but the thought that they could weasel something out of me that would help the Germans bring down another bomber crew was intolerable. I resolved to resist them until the last possible moment. I said a prayer as I entered the room, asking God to give me strength. My nemesis asked the question, I gave my standard reply, and then the blows started. This time they made me stand between the two guards so that one of them could knock me with the butt of his rifle towards the other who would catch me, and then use his gun to bat me back to the first one. I was batted back and forth, back and forth, until I lost my balance and fell to the floor. They yelled at me to get up. I tried, but there was simply nothing left. I lay motionless on the floor. They kicked me again and again, I don't know how many times, but I do remember that they finally dragged me from the room and down the stairs to my cell. I was too woozy from the beating to even stand up, so I lay crumpled on the floor, crying like a small child who'd been badly hurt. I never thought I would cry like that, but I hurt everywhere and wondered how much more I could take. I figured that I would probably die in the next interrogation because I just didn't see how I could stand any more beatings. The pain and despair were so overwhelming that I just lay on the floor sobbing. When I finally ran out of energy to cry, I lay still for a few moments and then prayed out loud to ask the Lord to help me endure this. I was in deep despair—at the end of my reserves. Almost immediately a very warm feeling came over me and filled my whole body. It was as if I heard Him say, "Hold on, I am with you." I knew then that somehow I would be okay, and I was able to close my eyes and go to sleep.

I never saw my interrogator again. For the next few days I huddled on the floor, the cold cement sapping more than just my body heat; it was as if life itself was draining out of me. I no longer had the strength to sit in the chair or even shiver to create internal body heat. I reluctantly ate the morsels of bread they offered and sipped the water carefully. My kidneys were so damaged that when I could urinate, there was blood in it. I could no longer walk upright, so I hobbled like an old, decrepit man as I struggled to go between the bathroom and my cell. Then one day the guards came in and grabbed me by the nape of my neck and took me out to a truck that was waiting in the courtyard. There were several other prisoners on board, a few Russians and some Americans, but no sight of my crew. When the truck started forward we talked quietly to each other and I asked them if they'd heard anything about my crew. I don't know where they got their information, but they told me that I was the only one to survive. A new wave of despair washed over me as I thought about my fallen crewmates. After traveling perhaps ten or fifteen miles we came to a train yard where we were lined up with hundreds of other prisoners to board a German train. I wondered wearily where our next stop was. At least I was with other Americans and I didn't feel quite so alone.

Having worked for the Union Pacific Railroad before the war, I expected to be loaded onto a large American-style passenger train. Instead, they crammed us into a narrow-gauge freight car that was so small that we all had to stand up or be squashed underfoot. It was late in the afternoon and cool outside, but within just a few minutes it became oppressively hot in the car from all the people crammed into such a confined area. I could see by the uniforms that there were several Americans, but I looked in vain to find a member of my crew.

We were on the train for several days and it may have been the first time in my life that I slept standing up. Everyone just sort of leaned against each other and slumped until we couldn't go any lower, and then fell asleep. When the train pulled onto a siding to take on water or fuel the sliding doors would be opened a bit, which let a welcome breath of fresh air in, but they never let us get off the train. At one siding two prisoners fell out when they opened the doors, and the German Shepherd guard dogs attacked them so ferociously that they both died.

The stench in the car was overpowering, particularly since there was no place to go to relieve ourselves. When one of the prisoners had to go he would let out a strangled sort of scream and say "I'm sorry, but I just can't hold it any longer," and he'd go in his pants. There was nothing else you could do and when the fellow next to you went you just had to bear it.

I don't know how long they made us go without water, but we were getting desperate. I was so dehydrated that my tongue started to swell, which made it even more difficult to breathe. On one of the stops we pleaded with the guards to get us some water, so they went forward to the engine and came back with some rusty water from one of the boilers. It was the color of a copper penny from the rust. I looked at it and thought, "I can't drink it, I'd sooner die." I dipped my finger in the water and rubbed it on my tongue, but I did not swallow. I was determined to hold out until we made it to wherever we were going. By this time several of the men slumped to the floor and couldn't get up. There was groaning and crying and pleading. We had to concentrate really hard to shut out the cries or they would make us go crazy. When some of the guys fell to the floor they were nearly crushed to death because there was just no place to put our feet or to move. When we finally got to our destination, they ordered us to get out quickly and we did our best to step over the men who had fallen to the floor to avoid killing them. I never did find out what happened to those men.

What a marvelous thing to breathe fresh air again. I filled my lungs and relished the taste of the outside air. There were times when I really thought we might suffocate on the train, so it was a huge relief to have room to stand in the open without being crammed against another person. The guards ordered us to line up in groups of four and stand at attention. When we heard that, everybody laughed because we were in no condition to stand fully upright at all, let alone at attention! After assembling us by groups and columns, they marched us up a dirt road and then tried to make us run, but we could only go a short distance before men started falling to the ground. Almost in unison we somehow made the decision to slow back down to a walking speed and take the consequences. The guards just sort of shrugged and let us go at a more realistic pace. Just when I thought I had to stop or die, we reached a compound with a barbed wire fence around it and guard towers in each corner. We went inside and were herded into barracks. Everybody was dead-tired from little or no sleep, and we wanted to fall to the ground in the worst way, but to do so would be to sit in our own waste, which was also a horrible thought. Some of us fell to a kneeling position so we could take the weight off our feet and lower back. Eventually the guards showed a shred of human decency by taking us in groups of five to a shower room where they turned the water on. It felt wonderful to feel water on my face and to gulp down as much as I could. I could have stayed under the shower forever, but I suspected the Germans' "kindness" wouldn't last long, so I stripped off my clothing and washed my body and my clothes as fast as I could. Some of the men were so exhausted that they just stood there in their clothes. This turned out to be a mistake because before they knew it the water was turned off and we were ordered to put our soiled clothing back on. I felt fortunate to have been able to clean some of the stench and soil out of the fabric.

As we got back to the barracks, sloshing in our wet clothing, the air raid horns started blaring. The guards ordered us out of the building and marched us into an underground tunnel. They told us to shut up and say nothing. While we were sitting there in the dark one of the guards said in broken English, "How does it feel to be bombed by your own bombers?" Just then the bombs hit outside, creating such a monstrous blast that my ears went deaf for some time. A massive cloud of dust rolled through the tunnel and we had to shut our eyes and cough to clear the dust out of our throats. Since we knew the routine our bomb crews would follow, it was inevitable that there would be additional bombs coming, and we all prayed that the next payload wouldn't come any closer. For the first time in my life I hoped that the American bombardiers would miss the "objective" and turn out to be bad shots on this one mission. Everybody else must have thought the same thing because we actually found the strength to laugh about it as they marched us back to the barracks after the bombing run ended.

We stayed in this camp for about three days before being split up. Some of us were sent back to the same dirt road for a forced run back to the railway terminal. I had barely started to heal from my beatings and it felt good to be able to stretch my arms and legs. My mind revolted at the thought of getting back on one of those stinking, stifling box cars, but they didn't ask what I thought, and they quickly shoved us into another cramped railroad car. Fortunately, it wasn't quite as crowded as before. In fact, there was enough room that if half of us stood close together in one end of the car, the other half could sit on the floor with their backs to each other to take a nap or rest. We took turns standing and sitting. Plus, with this much room we could actually find an occasional hole in the side of the car to relieve ourselves. What a wonderful change from the first leg of our journey.

This segment took about seven days and the only food they gave us was the now-infamous black bread with sawdust. They didn't provide any water, only coffee. Because of my religious convictions, I refused to drink the coffee at first, but eventually I had to drink it or die. Even though I had promised to live by the "Word of Wisdom" in happier days, I felt that the Lord had preserved my life thus far for a purpose and that it was wisdom now for me to make this compromise. Soon I learned to live on coarse black bread and watered down coffee. We had no idea where we were going except that the guards made it sound like it was a long way off. The duration could have been considerably shorter if we hadn't been shunted to sidings periodically to wait for a high-speed troop train to go past. In fact, our train moved aside for everything. A herd of filthy Allied prisoners was a lot less important to the Germans than either freight trains or passengers, and they treated us with the contempt that befitted such a status.

At each end of the box car there was a very small window, high up on the wall, and some of the taller men could stand on their tiptoes and look out. I'm not very tall, so I had to settle for what they told me. Of course, the foremost question on our minds was, "Where are they taking us?" but a few quick glimpses of an unfamiliar countryside really didn't give much of a clue.

After a week of travel on this second leg of our journey the train finally came to a stop. When the Germans slid the heavy doors open, the sunlight nearly blinded us and we squinted as we jumped out of the car onto the ground. Our legs were so stiff and sore from standing half the time, and sitting with folded knees the other half, it was only natural that they buckled when we hit the ground. This did not please our German guards, half of whom had well-trained guard dogs at their sides. When we fell or stumbled the dogs lunged at us, snarling and baring their teeth, which brought us to our feet in a hurry. Once all the prisoners were off the train the guards made us stand at attention while they took an inventory of this new group of non-coms[1] and enlisted men who had the misfortune to become prisoners of war. As we stood unmoving, with eyes forward, our gaze fell on the commanding officer who stood in the center of the compound. He was really something to behold. He wore highly polished black leather boots that reached above his knees, a magnificent full-length black leather trench coat, and matching leather gloves. His high arched hat lent an air of authority to his stern face, and his chest displayed an impressive array of shining medals. He held a leather strap in his right hand and the tattered ends showed that he'd used it frequently. He paced around slapping the strap against his left hand, causing the leather to give such a sharp retort that I almost winced each time it sounded. The guards came and went, busily collecting information about each of us, then reporting everything to their leader. Their behavior was sharp, efficient and imposing, and only a fool would think to cross them.

Eventually they divided us into four columns and ordered us to march shoulder to shoulder up a tree-lined road. The pine forest was beautiful, and it was refreshing to see the autumn colors of the underbrush. It was late September now, so the air was pretty brisk, but it felt wonderful to smell the forest air and to feel the breeze and sun on my face. In some ways it reminded me of the trips I'd taken up the canyons that feed into the Salt Lake Valley, although the rounded hills of Germany were nothing compared to the rugged Wasatch Mountains of Utah. Still, the sight and smell of the forest had the odd effect of helping me feel somewhat closer to home. It also felt great to be able to move my legs and arms again after being crowded in a train for a total of ten days. The stiffness in my joints soon disappeared as my muscles heated up from the exercise. The biggest problem was that we were all pretty hungry and thirsty, so we couldn't move very fast, which kept the guards yelling at us the whole way. We did the best we could.

After about four or five miles of marching, we came to a clearing in the forest, which turned out to be our new home. In the center of the clearing was a large military compound, surrounded by a heavy wire fence. The most prominent feature of the camp was four wooden guard towers, approximately forty feet high, in each corner of the compound. Each tower was occupied by at least two German soldiers, a floor mounted machine gun, and a powerful-looking spotlight. It looked to me like the guards in the tower could see all the areas inside the compound from their elevated vantage point, and had an unre-stricted view of the one hundred foot clearing that separated the prison fence from the forest. As we drew closer to the compound I saw that there were fifteen or twenty guards marching around the perimeter of the fence. Each of these perimeter guards had a rifle slung over his shoulder as well as a German shepherd dog by his side. It was all pretty intimidating.

The gates to the single entrance of the compound swung open as we arrived and the guards who accompanied us from the train station ordered us to march into the drill area in the center of the compound. At this point the camp seemed to come alive as resident prisoners poured out of the barracks to look at the new arrivals. They stood at a discreet distance from our group, watching as the German Camp Commandant came out to address us. His confident expression and crisp bearing told us that he enjoyed his job. After a short briefing about prison rules and policies the Germans issued each of us a new set of dog tags with a German I.D. number stamped on it. My new identity was Prisoner Number 3327 KGF LGR 4 D LW. I was instructed to wear the German tags around my neck at all times, along with my G.I. tags. One of the German officers who spoke broken English assigned each of us to a barracks. I was told to report to Compound Number 3, Barracks Number 3. With that, the guards turned and saluted the Commandant, and after he made his exit, dismissed us. Only then did the resident prisoners come and welcome us to the camp, and help us sort out which way to go.

DIAGRAM OF PRISON CAMP

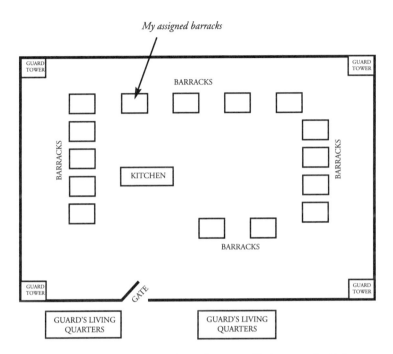

Each Guard Tower was stocked with a machine gun and high intensity flood lights.
The perimeter was surrounded by double rows of wire fence.
There were 50 to 75 men per barracks.

While I wasn't overjoyed to be in a concentration camp, it was great to hear the prisoners speaking freely to each other in English. I thought to myself that it was a lot better living here among my fellow countrymen than living in isolation back in the cold cement dungeon under the guard of my earlier tormentors.

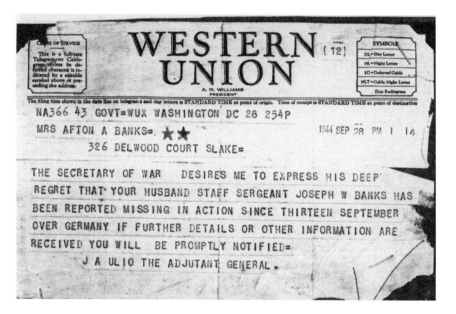

A telegram sent to Afton 15 days after our aircraft was destroyed.

NOTE

1. As a staff sergeant, I was a non-commissioned officer. On a B-17 bomber the pilot, copilot, bombardier, and navigator were all commissioned officers, with a rank of lieutenant or higher. The rest of the crew were enlisted men or non-coms. The Germans treated officers who were taken prisoner far differently than they did the rank and file prisoners. For example, I've had occasion to talk to a number of officers who were taken prisoner and none of them were interrogated the way I was, and their camps were far more comfortable than ours.

CHAPTER 6

Prisoner of War

When I entered the barracks, I was introduced to the twenty other men who would share their small room with me. Our living quarters weren't even as big as the living room and bedroom in the house where Afton and I lived in Salt Lake City, yet twenty of us were crammed in there. Before I could sit down to get my bearing the other prisoners started peppering me with questions about how the war was going, where I flew out of, where I was shot down, and what kind of aircraft I served on. The men were desperate for information about the outside world, and they discussed every little detail I could give them about our base camp in Foggia, or about the progress of the Allied war effort. I was really tired from the march and wanted to lie down and rest, but these guys were so pleased to have someone new that I kept trying to answer their questions for several hours into the night.

I wanted to know how long each of them had been a prisoner of war, and what it was like. Some of the men had been in the camp for almost a year, others just a few months. When some of the guys tried to answer my questions, others would interrupt to start asking me questions again. I soon figured out that there would be plenty of time for me to figure out what prison life was like, since time was something these guys seemed to have plenty of.

The Germans did not issue prisoners new clothing, so everyone was wearing the uniform they were shot down in. I was self-conscious because of the odor on mine, but the other prisoners' clothing smelled just as bad. Some of the uniforms were threadbare and stained, with holes in the knees or elbows. At any rate, no one said anything to me about the body odor or condition of my uniform.

After the group broke up the men came over one by one to welcome me. Although some of them acted nervous or withdrawn, most were very friendly. One man stood much taller than the rest. The others called him Focke-Wulf 190. He was a fighter pilot who had shot down more German aircraft than any other prisoner in the camp. He had a huge bushy red beard and mustache, and he spoke with a deep raspy voice that danced with delight when he told a funny story or joke. He was a jovial man and it was easy to enjoy his influence in the group. I could see that he was something of a natural leader since he was the one to assign me a bunk. Focke-Wulf was obviously someone who would play an important part in my life in the weeks and months to come.

It felt great to be back among people who spoke English and who could relate to the experience of flying in combat and being taken as a prisoner-of-war. Even though we'd been trained on what to do if our aircraft went down, there was no way to really understand how frightening and demoralizing it could be unless you'd lived through it yourself. While each of these men had their own unique story to tell, we could all relate to the anxiety that the others had felt when they found themselves at the muzzle-end of a German rifle. I looked forward to getting to know everyone better and to perhaps try and make sense of everything that had changed in my life.

I was assigned to an upper bunk that had a mattress made out of paper and cardboard, with no springs or other padding. My bunk-mate was Bob Salmon from North Dakota, who had arrived just a few days earlier, and he and I really hit it off right from the start. We were about the same age and had a lot of the same interests, including a passion for automobiles and sports. His aircraft had been shot down by Triple A, and he had to bail out before his aircraft exploded. We swapped stories about our welcome from the local citizenry, and I actually found myself laughing as I told him about the guards stepping on the cords of my parachute to trip me. It wasn't funny when it happened, but Bob laughed when I told him how I wanted to jump up and deck the guards who tormented me. What a relief to be able to talk about what I'd been through.

Another fellow in a neighboring bunk was a soft-spoken married man from Florida who was a bit older than the rest of us. Although Roland didn't say a lot, he liked Bob and me and the three of us were soon very good friends. Finally, a couple of weeks after I arrived, another airman named Lloyd Alburn was assigned to our barracks and soon joined our group. Lloyd was from Medford, Oregon and had lied about his age to get in the Army Air Forces, so he was the youngest in the group. We sometimes called Lloyd by his nickname, Rusty, because of his thick red hair. The four of us talked freely with each other and it was great to have people in whom I could confide and share my feelings about my family and friends, and my dreams for the future. In many ways, our dreams were all we had to keep hope alive, so we talked for hours at a time about our past and what we hoped would happen in the future when the war was over.

There were a lot of personalities in our barracks; some who were easy to like, others who were annoying. It turned out that Focke-Wulf was one of the people who caused me some distress. Not because he was mean or domineering, but because he was a show-off who liked to brag endlessly about his sexual exploits with women. No matter what the subject was, he'd find some way to turn the discussion to his favorite topic, and then regale everyone with his stories. Some of the men seemed to hang on every word, laughing uproariously when he'd tell a dirty joke or find some way to demean one of the women he'd supposedly been with. I eventually concluded that most of his stories were inventions of a very active imagination, but it often angered me to hear him talk that way about women. I wasn't a prude, but I had simply been raised to treat women with respect, and to keep intimate moments private. I came to hate it when the men would try to "one up" each other because it inevitably filled my mind with images that were hard to shake. Of course Focke-Wulf saw to it that no one ever topped his stories, so even though I enjoyed his cheerful and positive attitude, he and I never really became friends.

Another person who stands out in memory was an older man who was very literate (he spoke German fluently) but who complained constantly. He complained about the food, about the progress of the war, about the rest of us in the barracks, about the fact that he never seemed to get as much food as everyone else, and on and on. Sometimes he made people so mad they'd pick a fight with him just to get him to shut up for a few days. Inevitably he'd lose these matches and go sulk in his bed, but before long he was carping again, driving everyone crazy.

For the most part, I liked everyone in our barracks and was treated well by my fellow prisoners. Yet it was hard to keep twenty people in the same room day after day, with nothing to do but sit around and talk to each other, and not have a disagreement once in a while. To minimize the conflict most of us divided into groups with the guys we liked best. My foursome spent most of our time with each other since we seemed to have the same value system and type of goals we wanted to pursue when the war was over. Even when we were outside we stuck to each other like glue. If anybody gave a member of the group trouble, the other three would come to his rescue. Sometimes trouble meant that some of the guys in other barracks went looking for a fight, and would use any pretense to start something. If I accidentally bumped a fellow on the exercise ground, he might challenge me to a fight on the spot. When Bob, Roland, and Rusty showed up at my side, however, he would back down. Perhaps these prisoners wanted to stir things up for no other reason than to create a diversion from the tedium of prison life. It was so boring that we all looked for anything to make life a little more interesting—including fights, grudges, and arguments. There really was nothing to do during the day, since our exercise time was restricted to just a few hours out of doors every other day, and there was no work for us to do other than clean our part of the barracks and help with food service once in a while.

Many of the men in the camp had serious wounds that had not healed properly. Several of the guys in my room had to use walking canes and sticks because of injuries to their legs inflicted when their aircraft was shot up by enemy fire. They desperately needed medical attention, but none was offered by the Germans. It bothered me that the guards could see how much pain they were in as easily as we could, but none of them offered help, even when it was requested.

One of the biggest problems we prisoners faced was dysentery. This was a result of the poor quality of food we were given. The malady was characterized by diarrhea and a persistent desire to relieve oneself, even when there was nothing in the stomach. I watched as one of our room-mates twisted and turned in agony from the severe cramping in his stomach and bowels. Of course he was soon dehydrated, which led to a fever that added to his misery. It was pathetic to see him alternate between cold chills and profuse sweating as his body tried to fight off the dysentery.

As more and more people came down with dysentery some of the men were so weak they just laid in their bunks all day long and slept. That made them even weaker. Others would run to the end of the hall ten or twenty times a day to try to find relief, even though our meager diet meant that there was very little they could pass.

It was hard to be pleasant when we felt terrible. Most of us were still young enough to remember that it had only been a few years since our mothers cared for us and pampered us while recovering from a wound or wrestling with a debilitating illness. Yet here, some of the men were slowly dying with no one to give the help they needed. It was all very disheartening.

I wanted to stay close to the Spirit of the Lord, but it was pretty tough because of the constant profanity and dirty jokes and stories. There were many times when I wished for a copy of the scriptures to turn to for relief, but the Germans had taken everything from me. It was tedious with nothing to do but sit around and talk. We eventually heard everyone's stories many, many times. If only there were some books to read, or a radio to listen to, or jobs to be done. But there weren't. The Germans simply left us to our own devices most of the time, as long as we didn't cause any trouble. They certainly weren't interested in making our lives interesting or worthwhile. It was no wonder some of the men withdrew emotionally, hardly ever speaking at all.

The small shrapnel wound I'd received in my wrist when our aircraft blew up had never really healed. At first I thought of it as nothing more than an annoying scratch. But one morning I awoke to find my wrist all swollen and red. This condition worsened from day to day until eventually the redness extended clear up my arm. The skin started to peel off, leaving a running sore that oozed infected puss. It hurt so much that I couldn't sleep at night. The wound was constantly weeping, and it smelled so bad that it was making the other men sick. One morning I took my shirt off and saw large, menacing-looking red streaks going up my arm and over my shoulder towards my chest. Roland said it looked like gangrene to him. He and Bob helped me cross the compound to the guardhouse where we showed the guards how bad my skin was. One of the guards immediately escorted us to their doctor in the staff barracks outside of the compound. The doctor looked at it with alarm and grabbed my hand to make a closer examination. Just the touch of his hand hurt so terribly that I let out an involuntary shriek. He looked me straight in the eyes and said through a translator that I must have the arm amputated immediately or I would die. My arm hurt so badly that I couldn't imagine facing the pain of surgery, so I asked him what kind of anesthetic he would use. Reaching in his drawer, he pulled out a small stick and told me to put it in my mouth and bite down. That was the only thing available. When asked what kind of instruments he would use, he pulled out a pocketknife about four inches long. I looked at my buddies and they just shook their heads and looked back at me. I told the doctor I would have to think about it. He told me that there wasn't anything to think about since I would either lose the arm or I'd lose my life. He wanted to proceed immediately to save my life. To emphasize his point, he drew my gaze down to my arm to remind me that all the skin was gone from the wrist to the elbow, and the infection was spreading from there up to my shoulder and out into my chest. It was one of the worst cases of gangrene he'd ever seen, and he was concerned that it might be too late already. Still, I couldn't bring myself to trust him, so I told him again that I'd have to think about it. He gave me until the next morning and said that after that it would be too late to do anything about it.

When I got back to the barracks all my roommates tried to talk me into letting him cut my arm off, but I had the dread feeling that I wouldn't make it through the operation alive. Finally, I asked them if they would all pray for me. This request took everyone by surprise and most of them stammered something like, "Sure, we'll pray for you, but is there some special way to do it?" I think everyone had privately said mental prayers in battle asking for help, but few of these men had ever said a formal prayer and they were embarrassed because they didn't know how. I was in so much pain, though, and so frightened of losing my arm that they were willing to do anything to help, so they let me teach them how to say a simple prayer. Some asked who to pray to. I told them briefly about my beliefs in God and Jesus Christ. I also told them they could pray to their own God if they believed differently. I explained that I believed that their faith could help to save my arm and my life. Eventually they all said okay, they'd do it, but they wanted me to start out. For the first time in camp I was able to pray out loud and it was wonderful. I felt the Spirit of the Lord come into the room in a powerful and comforting way. These terrific men, who could be so coarse and unrefined, started speaking to God with sincere hearts and out of love for me, their friend. Their prayers were simple, with common phrases like "Please, God, help Joe to know what to do," or "Joe's a pretty decent guy, won't you help him live through this?" A frequent sentiment seemed to be, "We've all been through so much, God, please don't let it end here for Joe—he wants to go back to his wife and son."

I know He heard their prayers and I wept with appreciation. I was still scared, but I finally felt the Spirit and was at peace again. That night the room was quiet when the lights were turned out, and even Focke-Wulf refrained from telling his off-colored stories.

I didn't sleep very well because the arm continued to hurt intensely. When morning arrived my three buddies took me over to the doctor where I found him getting things ready for the operation. When I took my shirt off, however, he looked at me with a startled expression. When I looked down at my chest I was surprised to see that the ugly red lines of the infection were gone and the swelling had gone down somewhat. The doctor declared that it was a miracle and that he would never have believed such a thing was possible. He told me that we could wait another day to see what would happen.

When I went back to the barracks and told the guys what had happened they all let out a cheer. I asked them to please remember me each night in their prayers and most of them promised they would. Later, many of them came up and told me that they had never prayed before that night, but they had continued to do so from that day on.

Each day after that my arm felt a little better, and the doctor finally declared that surgery would be unnecessary. He started wrapping it in newspaper because there were no bandages in the camp. I didn't like this very much, though, since the ink would leach into my raw flesh—so much so that sometimes you could make out the words on my skin. Rather than risk another infection, I left the arm exposed to the air. It took several weeks to heal, but eventually all traces of the gangrene and the original wound were gone. Any scars and discoloration were indiscernible. I said many a prayer of thanks and acknowledged this as yet another miracle where the Lord saved my life. There's simply no other explanation.

It was also good for my soul to be able to talk with other people about prayer, and to occasionally say a verbal, rather than silent, prayer. It was hard to keep my deepest feelings private without ever talking about them, and because of this illness I was able to let the other people in the room know how I felt. I didn't try to be overzealous in talking to them about religion, but I just wanted them to sense that God was important in my life. Bringing it all out in the open made it easier for me to feel the Spirit of the Lord.

After having a remarkable spiritual experience like this, I hoped that it would mark a permanent change in my life for the better. Unfortunately, it didn't take long to settle back into the routine of camp life. The morning after being released from the doctor's care, I was awakened by a guard and his dog, just like on every other morning. They threw the door open while shouting "Geh raus, Geh raus, Geh raus!" which I think means "hurry up, hurry up, hurry up." Everyone had to jump out of bed instantly or run the risk of being attacked by the dog. An attack only happened a few times, but the results were gruesome, with the offending prisoner suffering from the savage bites of the German shepherd's teeth. Of course the prisoner couldn't hurt the dog in any way or he ran the risk of getting beaten by the guards.

We had just a few minutes to get dressed and then line up at attention in front of our barracks for the guards to count us. If the count was short, the dog and guard would go back and search the room for the missing man. The straggler would be dragged from the room and made to stand at attention in the compound long after the rest of us were dismissed. If he was a repeat offender he would sometimes be placed in solitary confinement, with more limited food rations.

When everyone was accounted for, the guard would march to the center of the compound and salute the officer of the day with the straight arm "Heil Hitler" salute, and the officer would return the "Heil" and then receive the prisoner count. Next there would be announcements. Some days there was nothing, other days they'd inform us that we were to be punished with short rations, or no outside privileges for the day. These punishments were for rule infractions such as prisoners fighting on the compound the previous day. Sometimes they ordered us to clean our rooms and the toilets, even though our regular duties required us to clean our rooms and the latrine anyway. Even the annoying announcements, like the loss of privileges or extra duty, gave us something to talk about, so we listened intently.

When announcements were over, we were dismissed with orders to return to our cramped room, where we'd sit and talk about the same things we'd talked about the previous day, and the day before that, and the day before that. Some of the men weren't very sociable and would just say "Hi." Once in a while, when the lights would go out, we could hear one of the men crying, but nothing was said since we all felt like crying at one time or another.

There were three special days each week when we got to go outside for a while. On a sunny day we'd go out, sit down on the ground, and take our shirts off to pick the lice and bedbugs from our clothing. During our brief interludes in the open air we would do our best to exercise, although the meager diet and lengthy periods of enforced idleness left us quite weak. Still, it felt great to walk around and smell the pine scent of the nearby forest. My friends and I would walk around the perimeter of the compound and look up at the guard towers. The barracks were arranged in four sections, in a horseshoe pattern, with the exercise and assembly area in the center. We were never allowed to go into a barracks building other than our own, so we didn't really get to know the other men in the camp very well. We lived in our own little world, completely isolated from one another.

When R & R was over, it was back to our room. Usually we had several hours outside, but it varied based on the mood of the Camp Commandant. We had no baths or showers, and no way to clean our teeth. I'd rinse some of the coffee water in my mouth and then rub my finger on my teeth to try to clean them. Most of the men didn't even do that. Eventually everyone's teeth were so yellowed with stains that it looked like we had rust on them. We all had bad breath and body odor, but there was nothing that could be done about it, so we just had to bear it. We grew beards and long hair because there were no tools with which to groom ourselves. My beard was reddish-brown and scraggly.

The most popular part of our daily routine was chow time, even though it came just two times per day—brunch and dinner. The menu was simple and predictable: soup twice a day, along with some black bread and coffee. When it was mealtime the cooks would bring the big kettle of soup into our barracks and we'd eat our share from a small personal mess kit that included a fork and spoon, (no knife, of course, since it could be used as a weapon). The cooks made the soup out of dandelion greens and anything else they could find. The bread was so dry from being laced with sawdust that it stuck in my throat. I found it very difficult to eat anything during my first few weeks in camp. But as I got used to it, it actually started to taste pretty good. The soup provided some warmth, which really helped as the days and nights grew colder. Our camp was far up in the northern part of Germany near the Polish border, and close to the North Sea, so the weather was often bitter cold. The nights were always below zero degrees Celsius (the freezing point of water), and the humidity made the cold even more difficult to bear since it penetrated our clothes and blankets. I even came to like the heavy bread since it would swell inside our stomachs from the soup, providing temporary relief from hunger. There was never enough to keep us properly nourished and we were hungry most of the time. No one had anything that resembled a belly or extra body fat, and we resented the meager diet. Food was one of the main topics of discussion in the tent, and sometimes our conversations turned into fantasies of wonderful meals we'd enjoyed in the past. Even though all of my roommates were products of the Great Depression when food was sometimes hard to come by, none of us had ever experienced this kind of deprivation. Some of the hotheads vowed to take revenge on the Germans when the war was over. I didn't know at the time just how desperate Germany's food situation was. It wasn't until later that we learned that we were as well fed as most of the local citizenry, perhaps better. But in spite of that, we all continued to lose weight from the lack of food with real substance. The only way I could keep track of my personal weight loss was to count the number of extra holes I had to punch in my belt to keep my pants up. I used the fork in my mess kit to make the adjustment.

The only beverage they served during a meal was coffee, which I liked least of all. I'd dilute it with as much water as possible, and I found that it really did help to ease the hunger pangs during the eight to fifteen-hour intervals between meals. The other prisoners couldn't understand why I diluted it, but I had my private reasons. It was always noisy during brunch or dinner, but in spite of that I started a habit the first day I was there of closing my eyes and saying a silent prayer before eating my food. I was self-conscious, of course, but I soon found that three or four other men did the same thing. The rest of the guys in the room just started eating as soon as the soup was served, but they never bothered those of us who did take time for a prayer.

Each of us took turns serving the soup, but no matter how careful we were, someone always complained that someone else got a bigger serving. That would start a major argument at virtually every meal and soon everybody was griping. Fighting and bickering were inevitable with dozens of men cooped up in a drafty barracks with nothing to do.

Another problem was how to wash our mess kits and utensils together in a small bucket of water—a breeding ground for disease. Sometimes the water would be so black by the time it was my turn that I would pass on using the water altogether, and instead get permission to go outside and just rub my utensils and pan in the dirt. This was a trick I learned in Boy Scouts. Dirt is just dirty, but filthy water shared by so many men can transmit disease.

Dysentery remained a constant problem, characterized by intense stomach cramps and diarrhea. I managed to avoid this malady the entire time I was in camp, which I attributed to the prayers I said over my food. But most of the men got it and it was awful to see them suffer as they moved about, nearly folded in half and holding their stomachs. On the days when they couldn't make it out for roll call we'd sometimes try to cover for them by packing ourselves really tight in the line. One of the men would answer for the missing prisoner and then sneak down behind the rest of us to his own position in the line. If the guards found out about this trick they'd drag out the sick prisoner, threatening to turn the dog loose on him and we'd all have to stand there while it was sorted out. When our subterfuge was discovered we were all punished by having our exercise restricted or food withheld.

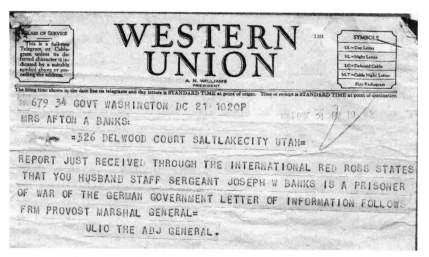

More than a month passed before notice was received at home in the United States that I'd been taken prisoner.

One of the questions on my mind the first day I arrived was whether or not it was possible to escape from the camp. There were a number of reasons for this curiosity. First, I didn't relish the thought of spending time as a prisoner of war. I didn't like losing my freedom and being subject to the whims of our captors. Second, we had an obligation to try to disrupt the enemy's war effort as much as possible, and a well-planned escape attempt would force the Germans to assign more soldiers as guards. I didn't really discover a third reason until I'd been in camp for several months. I learned that the effort involved in planning an escape attempt provided the people involved with something to do. It created a diversion in our otherwise boring existence.

To make it difficult for those who wanted to try and escape, the barracks were built on stilts with the floor about three feet above the ground. The Germans could more easily see if we were digging a tunnel to escape. While that was probably a good design for the captors, it made things particularly miserable for us, since it was very cold when the wind and snow whistled underneath the flooring.

In spite of the Germans' efforts to thwart any escape attempts, camp life was so tedious that it drove some of the prisoners who had been imprisoned the longest to take desperate measures for freedom, including figuring out ways to build escape tunnels under the fence. To build the tunnels, the prisoners had to find a place where they could pull up the floorboards and work in darkness. That was difficult, since every night the guards would fire up the four giant spotlights that were mounted in the guard towers at each corner of the compound, and they would swing the lights back and forth over the grounds and on the barracks all night long until daybreak. We could see the lights constantly sweeping the grounds, even though there were wood shutters on our windows. To avoid detection, the prisoners had to find a location in the barracks where they could work in the shadow of the building and out of range of the spotlights. The work was tedious and frightening, since any unusual noise might startle a guard dog or prompt an unscheduled inspection. We posted a watch to warn of an impending search. The men would bring up a great deal of dirt in their nightly labor, which had to be dispersed around the camp the following day. In spite of all the obstacles, however, some men succeeded in building workable tunnels that extended beyond the wire fence.

I never tried to escape, but I knew some of the men who did. Their fate was always the same. As soon as their head would appear outside the compound, a guard would be waiting with one of the meanest dogs. If the prisoner made any attempt to run, the guard would either bayonet him or sic the dog on him. More than one man died while trying to escape. Those who were caught and returned to the compound were deprived of their shoes, which was really terrible in the winter months.

While it made sense that the Germans would eventually recapture most of those who escaped, it was almost impossible that they could know precisely the moment an escaping prisoner would appear from a tunnel. Impossible, that is, unless there was an informant. Eventually we wormed the name of the informant from one of the guards. It turned out to be a fellow prisoner in another barracks who decided to trade the name of his own countrymen in exchange for some more food and other privileges. His treasonous actions had led to more than one Allied death, so something had to be done. Eventually, lots were drawn and one of the prisoners killed him one night. We all watched solemnly as the Germans carried his body out. It was a sickening experience, but one that I felt had to be taken to protect the rest of us. Since we talked quite freely among ourselves, there was no telling what information he had given the Germans that could be used against those of us in prison, or even to help the Luftwaffe shoot down our own aircraft. I couldn't understand how anyone could betray his friends like that.

In practice, the escape attempts were the exception, not the rule. Most of us worked hard just to stay alive, and the cold and hunger were the two greatest enemies to survival. Besides building the barracks on stilts, which created a perpetual breeze under our feet, the rest of the building was built out of flimsy lumber with wide cracks between some of the boards. When the wind blew, we all felt it inside. Of course there was no insulation. For heat the guards would give each room a daily issue of two black bricks for the stove. Each brick was about half the size of a masonry brick used in home construction in the United States. They were made of something like charcoal, so they didn't really burn with an open flame, but they'd glow and smolder, putting out a fairly steady heat. The bitter cold nights were the most difficult to bear, so we started saving the brick issued for daylight hours to burn two bricks during the night when there was no sun to help warm the building. We were always rubbing our hands and legs trying to keep warm, and sometimes we'd spend the entire day curled up in our bed under the blanket.

Periodically we were given a few pieces of paper to write letters home, but we were warned that they would be censored. If we gave away too much information, the Germans told us the letters wouldn't be sent at all. So all I could say was something like, "I am fine, they treat me well, and the food is okay, but I miss you and love you and Randy." I wrote each week and sent them out, hoping the German government would mail them. I never received any mail in the nine months I was a prisoner, even though I later learned that Afton had written every day. It was so lonely not hearing from home, and I found myself worrying about what might happen to my family. I could never write about my concerns or my treatment, since that would guarantee that the censors would either punish me or hold my outbound letters.

Each prisoner was supposed to receive a Red Cross package once a month, which included cigarettes, candy bars, canned Spam, crackers, coffee, sugar, and C Rations. Unfortunately, we only received one package during the four months I was in the camp. Boy, was it great to have something besides black bread and soup! We had plenty to talk about that day, and it was interesting to watch how each of the other men in the room handled the small bounty of this Red Cross treasure. Some were so famished that they ate everything just as quickly as they could tear the wrappers open. Others carefully savored each bite, as if they were enjoying a great feast. I personally tried to stretch it out for more than a day, but eventually yielded to the temptation to just eat everything in a futile attempt to quiet the hunger in my stomach. I don't know what happened to all the other packages that were supposed to come to us, but we had our suspicions that the German guards got an extra nice meal once a month.

Probably the most valuable commodity in the kit was one that I didn't care to use personally—cigarettes. They were the universal medium of exchange, with more value in the closed environment of our prison camp than any amount of money. To the men who were smokers, a cigarette had the ability to quiet the pain in their stomach from hunger, and to quell the nicotine craving that they said was always with them. I saved and traded my cigarettes for other goods or food that a prisoner or guard might be willing to trade. Some men gave up their C rations for a pack of cigarettes, which meant I got extra nourishment at no cost to me. I felt kind of bad taking their food, but they were happy with the exchange and I was hungry. Other items to trade included articles of clothing, pencils and paper, or other valuable items like shoelaces. It was considered perfectly appropriate to hold out for the highest bidder, whether it was another prisoner or one of the guards. Cigarettes carried a premium value and were often the source of arguments and fights in the camp.

When you think about how much energy young men in their twenties have, it's a miracle that we survived the boredom and confinement. The Geneva Convention didn't allow the Germans to use us as forced laborers, and they honored that part of the agreement. I'm grateful for that, since the watery soup we had to eat would never have sustained us. Yet in some ways it would have been nice to have something to do. On at least one occasion the frustration turned ugly, and we heard that one of the men had been raped by someone in his room. The other men in the room dragged the perpetrator outside and almost beat him to death. These instances were rare, though.

We had only two toilets per barracks, which was a real problem with so much stomach distress caused by our poor diet. Once a week a wagon with a large sewage tank would pull up to our barracks to clean out the collection tank that served a couple of hundred men. The Germans would insert a long hose into the tank, put some type of gas in it, and then light a match. There would be a "poof" sound, which created suction that siphoned the sewage from the tank into the wagon. It smelled pretty bad for a while after the wagon left, but provided some diversion.

A frequent topic of conversation among the prisoners was the personality of the guards we had to deal with. Since they had seemingly unlimited authority over us, we had to learn to adapt to each guard to avoid getting punished. Sometimes you couldn't avoid making them angry, since some of them enjoyed having an excuse to abuse a prisoner. But some prisoners were more successful than others in getting along with the guards. From what I could tell, there were three types of guards in the prison camp.

A small handful of guards were unusually sadistic and cruel. This was the group of guards who would goad a prisoner into doing something foolish, then punish him for his insubordination. It was easy for them to do, since they could trip us, or yell at us for not cleaning our room properly, even though we'd spent hours working to get it as good as possible. Sometimes they'd just hit a prisoner with no apparent provocation. When he'd get up, angry and ready to defend himself, they'd really let him have it, and administer a fierce beating with their billy clubs or the butt of their rifles. Of course the guards were never wrong, so there was no point to appeal their punishment.

Most were just really arrogant and uncaring. Many of the guards were older men who had been washed out of the regular army for some reason—perhaps a physical limitation, lack of ambition, or sometimes a lack of mental capacity. I always thought that they were the kind of people who had been kicked around all of their lives, and now found themselves in a position of authority over defenseless Allied prisoners over whom they could lord their superiority. If they saw a prisoner suffering, what was that to them? We were the enemy, and they weren't required to do anything beyond the bare requirements of the Geneva Convention. It sometimes made a prisoner indignant when a guard would give a stupid order, but he had to follow through regardless, or face a beating or solitary confinement.

A few of the guards were pretty decent people. You could tell that some of the guards hated their job because they were good people in their pre-war life. These men loved their families, and were good neighbors and competent employees. Most of them wound up on prison detail out of sheer chance, and they tried hard to make the best of it. They manifested their good humor by being more patient with a prisoner who was sick or hurt, or speaking more softly to the prisoners and actually acting like we were human beings worthy of some basic respect.

We did our best to avoid the first group, ignore the guards in the second group, and befriend the nice ones. The way to do that was to engage them in conversation when possible. A few of the friendlier guards spoke broken English, so they would take time to talk with us. Since they were about as bored as we were, I think they enjoyed the diversion of talking to people from different countries. While they didn't particularly like prison life, some of them told me that they were happy to be on guard duty in a prison camp rather than on the front lines in Russia. Sometimes they'd sneak a German newspaper into our room, and then a roommate would translate it for us, since no one else could speak or write German. The papers were full of propaganda, telling of the great German victories and how their soldiers were smashing through the front lines and killing hundreds of thousands of Russian, American, and English troops, and shooting aircraft out of the skies by the hundreds. The papers always had a picture of Hitler and someone saluting him with the stiff-armed salute. We loved to hear the translation of the articles even when we knew that they were filled with false information. It was something different from our usual, bored conversations with each other.

After a while we learned to pick up some of the German words and we'd try them out on the guards. This usually prompted a fit of laughter. Apparently we weren't very good. We also enjoyed listening to the guards talk about America. To keep their morale high, their officers told them that Germany would have to occupy America after it won the war, which meant that each of the guards could count on being the mayor of an American city. Our star-struck guards took us aside and asked where a certain town was, like Cincinnati or Las

Vegas, and what it was like. We'd tell them outlandish stories about the city just for the fun of watching their reaction, sometimes pleasing them when we told them how grand their new assignment as mayor would be, sometimes disappointing them when we'd tell them fabrications about how terrible a place was.

As winter progressed into early November, the weather forced us to spend even more time indoors, and tempers flared more frequently. Not a day went by without someone getting edgy and blowing off steam. This usually involved an argument with another prisoner. The fight might be over politics or baseball, or who was the most beautiful movie actress in Hollywood, or other meaningless things like that. The topic really didn't matter; it was just an excuse to fight. It didn't take much to set some of the men off. I was often called on to help settle an argument. Some of the time I could talk to the contenders and calm them down, but other times they were so angry it was best just to leave them alone until they cooled off on their own.

The D-Day landings had taken place in June 1944, three months before I was shot down, so all of us knew that the Allies had started to close in on Germany. What we didn't know was how well the advance was going for the Allies. In November a new group of prisoners were brought in, and they gave us the good news that the Allied forces were making swift progress through France towards the German border. Many of them predicted that we would be liberated by Christmas. Since that was less than two months away, we were hopeful that the war would soon end, and we'd get to go home. By mid-December, however, the German guards proudly announced that the Wehrmacht had launched a massive counter-attack that was pushing the Allies back. This was so disappointing, even though we didn't know if we could believe them. It was emotionally draining to get our hopes up only to have them disappointed by news like that. Lloyd, Roland, Bob, and I decided not to talk about it anymore. Then we started to hear the concussions of artillery fire off in the distance and saw columns of tanks moving east past our camp. Since we were so close to the Polish border this could only mean that the Allies on the Eastern Front, the Russians, were getting close and might be in a position to rescue us soon. When we heard the staccato sound of Russian aircraft strafing German positions with their machine guns, we knew that the end was close.

One morning, one of the friendly guards pulled me aside and said that the Russian troops were advancing too close and so the German army was going to evacuate, leaving us there with a skeleton crew of guards. When I told that to the other men in the barracks they let out a shout. We were all cheered up at the prospect of being out by Christmas or New Year's Day. A couple of days before Christmas, however, the news took a terrible turn when the guards told me to start getting the men organized. The decision had been made to take us with them. Even though the Germans were terrified at the thought of being captured by the Russians, they still didn't want to let them have the prize of liberating a prisoner of war camp. I asked what kind of transport would be provided and they told me we'd have to go on foot. I protested that this was impossible, since most of the men were sick, we had only threadbare clothing, and our shoes were almost completely worn out. They just said, "That's too bad—now start getting things organized!" At this point I felt like I didn't have anything to lose, so I pleaded one more time, "We'll freeze to death without any coats or blankets to stay warm at night." The guards finally agreed that we could take one blanket for every two men. That was all we would get. When I asked about food they told me to not worry, that we would be taken care of.

One moment we thought we were on the verge of liberation, the next we were being forced to march back into the heart of Germany, in the one of the coldest winters on record. This particular batch of "good news" was delivered on Christmas Eve day. I don't know why the guards entrusted me with the job, but I passed the news onto the other prisoners in our barracks. I decided to pair the men up so that there would always be someone to watch out for the other. There wasn't really a lot more to organize since we had no possessions other than a mess kit and utensils.

Some of the guys decided to celebrate Christmas Eve surreptitiously, so they immersed the raisins and prunes they'd saved from the Red Cross package in a pan of warm water. The fruit fermented in the water, and when they took the lid off the odor filled the whole room. Since they hadn't told anyone, it was quite a surprise and it pleased most of the other guys. They watered down the mixture and gave each man a cup full. I didn't drink any, but shared my portion with my three buddies. Everyone was pretty pleased with their bootleg "alcohol."

That evening we joined in singing Christmas carols and talked about the Christmas story. It was also great to hear the familiar songs coming from the other barracks as well. While we didn't know what our futures would be, it was wonderful to pause and think of the great traditions that bound us all together. We all tried to settle in for sleep as best we could, and tried to enjoy the relative warmth of our room.

Trouble started about an hour later. Fermented juice in shrunken stomachs (that haven't been processing food or drink for a while) has an overpowering effect. Before long everyone was drunk. Some of the men started to throw up, and the pain in their bellies was so awful that they doubled over and started moaning and groaning. They said they thought they were going to die. By morning two of the men were in such agony that we had to call the guards and ask them for medical help. They dragged the men off to the dispensary, and the men never came back. We assumed that they had died, although the guards would never talk about it.

The following morning, December 26, 1944, the guards came in with their dogs and pointed their weapons at us. They shouted the familiar, "Geh raus, raus, raus!" We knew something bad was going to happen since they had bayonets mounted on their rifles. When we asked what was going on they told us that we were moving out that morning, so everyone had to get ready to go right away. That didn't take long, since all we had were the clothes on our backs, a blanket for every two men, and a mess kit. When the guards left for a few minutes I went to my bed and said a prayer, asking Heavenly Father to bless me to say the right thing to the other men so they wouldn't rebel and get themselves killed. Since the guards had chosen to communicate their orders through me, the men in the barracks were coming to me and my friends, asking what they should do. Some were hollering, others were crying, and some just stood there staring into space. We all knew that we were in no condition to go into the frozen snow and icy wind, yet it was that or be shot. After letting off as much steam as we dared, we went outside to meet our fate in a hostile land. It was quite a way to end the year of 1944.

CHAPTER 7

Eight Hundred Kilometers of Misery

Our ragtag group of emaciated, filthy men assembled on the drill grounds that cold, clear December morning. Half were hunched over from dysentery, many limped because of poorly healed battle wounds, and everyone shivered from the freezing cold weather. The guards assembled us into four columns and then gave the order to start marching. I'm not sure anyone would have obeyed if it hadn't been for the dogs and bayonets. I looked at Roland for some kind of reassurance, but he just shrugged. It seemed so hopeless. After all, most of us were wearing summer weight uniforms, with no coats or gloves, and we had to take turns draping the single blanket issued for every two men over our shoulders.

One of the men suggested that we start singing Christmas carols again to keep our spirits up. It proved to be a good idea, and before long our attitudes brightened and our muscles started to limber up from the exercise, which made moving a little bit easier.

There were a lot of mixed emotions among the men as that first morning wore on. Some were grateful to be out of the confinement of the barracks and to walk among the trees, smell fresh air, and feel the sun on their faces. Others were afraid that they'd die from exposure without coats or anything substantial to protect them from the elements. A few expressed an ominous foreboding that the Germans were taking us out into the forest to kill all of us in a mass murder. I worried how they would feed this many men on the move, since there were nearly 1,000 Allied prisoners. In spite of our worries, the guards ordered, "March!" so we marched.

At first our greatest concern was for our personal comfort, but when we passed through the first German town we learned that there was a far more potent threat from the local civilians. The destruction they'd endured at the hands of Allied bombers was unbelievable. Nearly every building had been blasted to rubble by English bombers. Instead of a city, all we saw were mounds of brick and mortar, with only an occasional wall here or part of a roof there. I didn't see a single undamaged building in the entire area. At first glance it appeared that everyone had evacuated, leaving the place deserted. But as we entered the city limits, people started to emerge from holes in the ground, and they were angry. The bombing had been so thorough that it had made everything above ground level uninhabitable. The only place the Germans could go was into the cellars, where they lived in gloom and squalor. It must have been suffocating to be stranded down there, choking on the dust that slowly sifted down on them, with no windows or chimneys to provide ventilation. When they saw us, the cause of their distress, they came up to taunt, spit, and scream at us with hateful, agonized looks on their faces. Many of them hit us with clubs and sticks. One old woman lifted her skirt, squatted, and urinated in front of us as a sign of her contempt. Some of the people would come up and hold out baskets of food only to snatch them away if a soldier tried to reach out. They didn't have much more to eat than we did—they certainly looked every bit as emaciated. But after living on our meager rations for the past few months the food they held out was tantalizing, and they loved to torture us with it. I think they wanted to lure us into an argument to give the guards a chance to hit us with their guns or turn the dogs loose on us.

On one occasion, a woman came up and spit in the face of a man in front of me. When he reached out instinctively to stop her, one of the guards stabbed his right arm with a bayonet, cutting a deep wound that bled profusely. We patched it up and he lived, but it taught us in unmistakable terms that no matter how demeaning or infuriating the treatment of the citizens was, we had to endure it and keep marching forward. After all, it was our bombs that had done this to them. It was a bitter cold winter and these poor people were left exposed in cellars with very little fuel or food. It was even worse knowing that there were only women and children in these cities. Most of the German men were serving in the German army. I hated to see little children exposed to the cold with little or nothing to protect them. Everyone in Germany, including American prisoners, knew what it felt like to be slowly starving.

It struck me that everything was so different down here on the ground than it had been up in the air. Back then, we flew a "mission" to destroy an "objective" so we could "minimize the enemy's ability to wage war." When our bombardier released the bombs, we could see the puffs of black smoke on the ground that indicated we were successful. Even more dramatic was when he would "walk the bombs in" by dropping them in sequence so that a line of black puffs appeared. From my new vantage point, as a prisoner climbing through the rubble on the ground, I could now see just how devastating such an attack is, and it was unsettling to realize that an "objective" often included someone's house. Although it was necessary for us to do what we did, it was tragic that the Nazi leaders made it so. In reality these people were victims of their own government and its decision to bring the whole world to war. Yet, even though we understood why the people resented us, this understanding didn't make being spit upon or clubbed any easier. We were defenseless.

Every city that had any kind of industry at all was totally destroyed. Some of the very small towns hadn't been targeted, however, so at least the people there had homes to live in. I was always glad to see that. Usually the women in these towns stayed inside with their children, but we could still see them staring at us from behind their curtains. It was a forlorn sight.

In some cases the people in the towns or cities joined the exodus. Everyone was frightened about being "liberated" by the Russians. Early in the war Hitler had signed a mutual non-aggression treaty with Stalin so that he could fight the English without having to worry about defending an eastern front against Russia. When he later unleashed a surprise attack on the Russians it was an outright betrayal of the treaty and the Russians hated the Germans for it. Plus, the fighting in Russia had been terrible beyond imagination, with untold human suffering, so Stalin made it well-known that his military intended to get their revenge by conquering as much territory as possible. Most of the people of Germany, including our guards, knew that it would be better to be captured by the English and Americans, who were slowly working their way toward the German border in the west. The mass migration we were involved in was one of the largest movements of people in human history.

On the first night out of camp we were ordered to sleep in an open field. I protested to one of the friendlier guards that we'd freeze to death without any kind of cover, but he just shrugged and told me that this was it—we simply had to sleep on the ground. There was still snow everywhere, so I knew we were in for a cold, wet night. When I asked one of the guards about a latrine he went and got a shovel for us to dig a large trench. As we settled to the ground some of the men started to take their wet boots off to dry their feet and rub some warmth into them. I tried to stop them; a frozen boot would be nearly impossible to put on the next morning. Some listened, but others went ahead. Sure enough, they had a terrible time the next morning. For dinner that night they passed out a boiled potato for every two men. In better times it wouldn't have been enough to even fight over, but now each tiny morsel was coveted, and no one let a single crumb fall to the ground without retrieving it. I shared my blanket and potato with my buddy in our informal foursome, Lloyd Alburn, who was a year younger than me. Lloyd was a real worrier who had difficulty adjusting to the deprivation we experienced in prison camp. If he didn't watch his attitude, he would slip into something of a whining depression that added to the natural misery of our condition. The rest of us in the group always tried to be cheerful with him and get him talking about home or other topics of interest to divert his attention from the things that discouraged him. On this night, he was obsessive about making sure he got his fair share of our small potato. He asked me to cut the potato in half, and watched like a hawk to make sure each portion was equal. To make absolutely certain he even took the trouble to measure it. All I could do was laugh, which embarrassed him, and then he apologized.

We found a tree to lean against, and then huddled close to each other to share whatever body heat we could generate. Most of the other teams did the same thing. Some used the blanket as a cover, as we did, while others put it on top of the snow to stay a little drier. Over the course of the march, Lloyd and I tried it both ways, but it didn't really make a difference since we were cold no matter what we did.

On a typical day we'd get up in the morning and start marching in silence. When the sun came out someone would start singing a song, and pretty soon most of the prisoners in that column would be singing along. One of the American prisoners was a great singer who had memorized every Mills Brothers song ever recorded. He worked with us until all the English-speaking prisoners within earshot learned the words and melodies. It really helped our spirits to sing great old songs like, "Down By The Old Mill Stream," "Daisy, Daisy," and "Moonlight and Roses." We also liked to sing the military anthems of the army, navy, and marines, as well as other patriotic songs that reminded us of home. While the four columns of prisoners were way too spread out to sing the same songs at the same time, I could hear different groups singing up and down the line. In our group there were probably forty or fifty singing at a time.

The Germans were puzzled about why we'd sing, and they asked how we could be so happy. Sometimes it was just a big front to make them think that they weren't getting to us, but it truly helped us to endure the long days and freezing nights. Singing has such a positive effect on a person's emotions, and I found it to be a powerful motivator to keep going.

On the third or fourth day of the march I saw some brown paper on the ground, which I picked up. As I unfolded the paper in my hands, an idea came into my mind. I asked one of the guards if he would give me a pencil, which he did, and on our next break I started to draw a map of Germany. I tried to remember everything I could from my school days and from the maps we saw in the briefing rooms back in Italy. Some of the guards helped with the details. From that point forward I took notes of such things as road signs indicating how many kilometers it was to the next town, the names of the towns and cities we passed through, and so forth. It was this map that helped me calculate how many kilometers we traveled and the general direction we were going. I don't know why I did it, perhaps because of natural curiosity, or maybe just to give my mind a puzzle to occupy the tedious hours of marching and resting. Somehow it helped to know that we were making progress.

I particularly remember February 14, 1945. In addition to being Valentine's Day, it was the longest day we marched. One of the guards told us that we'd traveled fourteen kilometers. By this point, six weeks after leaving the P.O.W. camp, we were all very weak from lack of adequate food and drink, and from the constant, bone-numbing cold.

I think even the guards could see that we were about done in, so they somehow arranged for us to stay in a barn. It felt like a five-star hotel, and for the first time in weeks we were able to take our shoes off and air them out. We stuffed them full of straw, hoping that it would absorb the moisture and keep them properly shaped if we stuffed it in hard enough. We could also crawl into the piles of straw ourselves, which provided some padding between our bony skin and the ground. Lloyd and I cuddled up to each other with our blanket and it was the warmest and best sleep we'd enjoyed since leaving the camp back in December. Everyone hated to leave the next morning. I would have preferred to stay there until the war ended, but our guards weren't ready to give up yet.

It was about this point that some of the guards told us that they'd heard rumors about the Americans advancing on Germany in the west. This caused them a lot of anxiety. We told them that it was obvious the war would soon be over, and we thought they should start thinking about giving up before Hitler had them all killed. I think some of them started to feel the same way because they began treating us a little bit better. Some even asked questions about how a democracy works and what it was like to live in America, where the government didn't take you away from your family to train you to be a soldier. So much of the time I hated these guys, but then they'd say something like that and I'd think to myself, "They don't know anything about life except what they've been taught by the Nazis." Then I'd feel sorry for them. Their anxiety about the outcome of the war caused them to lighten their harsh treatment of us. They weren't as quick to punish a straggler, and sometimes even offered a hand to help a prisoner up when he fell from exhaustion. The English-speaking guards sometimes gave us snippets of news when they received it. Everyone was growing more and more hopeful that we'd be liberated before long.

I became quite friendly with one particular guard, who occasionally gave me some lard out of a can that each of the guards carried on their belt. They told us that a spoonful of lard coated their stomachs and helped them keep warm when food was scarce. Since this particular guard spoke English pretty well, I asked him about his wife and family. He told me that his two sons had been taken away from him when they turned nine so they could go to a Nazi military boarding school. I thought at the time that the reason Germany was destined to lose the war is that whenever you break up the family you invite disaster on a society. I think this guard agreed with me, even though he couldn't say too much. Still, it was great to have the guards start acting a bit gentler with us.

Unfortunately, our luck took a turn for the worse when a group of Hitler's dreaded SS troops were assigned to guard us temporarily while some of our regular guards took a few days leave of absence to recuperate. Our regular guards were, for the most part, ordinary people who had been drafted to serve in their army. While they were loyal to Germany, they weren't fanatics.

The Waffen SS, on the other hand, were schooled from the time they were children to be sadistic and mean-spirited savages. By and large they were young and well fed, and they were like Hitler's attack dogs. They had been trained to subdue all internal dissent with remorseless attacks on their own people, so a bunch of worn out Allied prisoners were nothing to them. They were cocky and arrogant, and would do anything to provoke us—kicking, tripping, spitting and so forth. When one of our guys had more than he could take, and tried to protect himself or strike back, the SS rejoiced. They would beat the offender nearly to death, and then stand around and laugh as he writhed in pain on the ground. If anyone tried to get down to help him, they'd kick that person as well. It was a terrible sight to witness, but to resist them was futile in our weakened physical condition. We were beaten up no matter what we said or did.

It was a happy day when they got orders to go back to the Russian front, and we almost smiled inside to think that they'd be back in battle. As the SS formed into a column to start their march east, one of our prisoners shouted at them, "I hope our soldiers get you and never let you up again!" That enraged the SS and they came back and kicked him in the head and groin until he died on the spot. There was nothing we could say or do. I'll never forget the thud of their guns hitting his body, and his moans as he lay dying on the ground. Then there was silence, and we knew he was gone. When the SS knew he was dead, they held their fists high up in the air and shouted "Heil Hitler!" and went on their way, laughing and rejoicing. It was sickening, frustrating, maddening, and disheartening. Sometimes I wanted to kill them with my bare hands, other times I wanted to curl up and die. But there was never a chance to do either, since the order would soon come to march on, with the threat of dogs and bayonets to enforce our compliance.

As the days and weeks wore on, our meager diet of a shared boiled potato and a little water took an incredible toll on our health. Everyone I knew had dysentery, including me, and I had to stop ten or twenty times a day to try to relieve myself. Adding to the distress was the fact that we had no toilet paper, so we were forced to use leaves or straw or whatever else we could find, which left our skin raw and bleeding. Fortunately, I remembered something I had been taught at the Boy Scout National Jamboree I attended in Washington D.C. when I was fourteen years old, and it provided relief in these dark times. In one of the health classes, the instructor taught us that if we ever got diarrhea while out in the woods, it sometimes helped to eat some charcoal off the end of a burnt branch or stick. Since our guards were able to build small fires at night, I asked them if we could have the burnt remnants of their sticks, and they agreed. We'd pass this around the camp and eat a stick or two. Somehow, the charcoal coated our stomachs, which helped to relieve the dysentery. It wasn't a cure, but it helped for a while. Several of the prisoners died along the way, and we were all very weak. Probably the biggest thing that kept us going was the thought that the Americans and English were pushing towards us from the west.

Early one morning we were walking along a dirt road when all of a sudden some American P-51 fighters came screaming out of the sky at us. Everyone hollered to hit the ground, and Lloyd and I dove for a nearby ditch to take cover. Before it was over, three aircraft strafed us on two different runs, and they killed several of the men and wounded many others. When the skies were cleared we went back to the main group to see who we could help. The German guards were furious about the attack, and they refused to let us go back and help the wounded or bury the dead. They ordered us to march on while listening to the cries of our buddies behind us. It was absolute torture to walk away.

As January and February passed into the history books, our health was failing rapidly. When one of the men couldn't go any further, he'd drop in place, and some of us would put our arms underneath his armpits and lift him into a wagon pulled behind a horse. Usually these were the guys who had wounds that hadn't fully healed, or who required the use of a cane or walking stick. A brief reprieve on the wagon gave them some time to recuperate, and then they'd half-jump, half-fall off the wagon and start walking again. Invariably somebody else needed a spot by then anyway. Eventually there were too many sick and exhausted men to fit on the wagon, so people would just drop in their tracks. We tried to help them stand up and get going again, but if they didn't make an effort to stand we had to let them drop, or we'd go down as well. Sometimes the guards just left them where they lay, other times they'd drag them into a ditch by the side of the road. No one ever told us what happened to them, but I believe they were left to die of exposure or starvation.

With nearly a thousand men marching in a loose formation (the columns were long gone by this point), it was only natural to stay with our friends. Bob, Lloyd, and Roland walked next to me through the whole march. They were my best friends, the best a man could ever wish for. We did our best to protect each other and to keep each other's spirits up. It's sobering to describe how difficult the march was. Everyone was gaunt from starvation and dehydration, and while the guards tried to hurry us along, we staggered more than walked because our legs were so weak. Many of the men spent much of the time doubled over because of stomach cramps from dysentery, so they appeared to stumble because their center of gravity was forward of the natural walking position. In the first few weeks of the march, people complained about the inhumanity of the Germans in forcing us on a march like this, but after awhile it took too much effort to talk so we moved ahead slowly in silence. Occasionally I'd glance up at another prisoner and see that tears were streaming down his face because he was so discouraged. A lot of prisoners fell to the ground and would have stayed there to die if the guards hadn't prodded them with the muzzle of their rifles, or given them a kick until they struggled back to their feet. It's hard to tell how many lost the will to live as the weeks and months dragged on, but it seemed that the nightly encampment grew smaller with each passing day.

I don't know why I kept walking, other than because of the memory of my promise to Afton to try to make it home alive.

Sometimes as I walked along I could picture our last days together in Tennessee, and it was almost as if I could smell her hair again and feel the warmth of her hand on my face. On other occasions I had trouble remembering any of the people at home, and that really scared me. It all seemed so far away, and the only reality I could deal with was the unhappy one I was in at the time. It was at discouraging times like these that I leaned on my friends for emotional support.

There were times when I was so tired that I wasn't even afraid anymore. What could the guards do to me? Kill me? That would be a relief. Beat me? I was almost numb from the cold and fatigue. It was a small wonder that the four of us needed each other so much. While each of us became discouraged and ready to give up at some point, there never was a time when we were all down simultaneously. There was invariably someone to prod us along and try to cheer us up. Lloyd had the most trouble, and more than once I had to help him back to his feet. I remember him sobbing—pleading—to just leave him where he was so he could die in peace. But we'd made a pact to help each other, so I'd get Bob or Roland to help me get him standing, and we'd put his arms over our shoulders to get him going again. When he was finally able to walk on his own again, he was so grateful for our help, and he'd get sentimental telling us how much he appreciated and loved us. Because he was the one to share my blanket at night I think he felt closest to me. In some regards I thought of him as a younger brother who needed protecting and help. Perhaps that's why I cared for him so deeply.

I also turned to my Heavenly Father in prayer nearly every step of the way. There were times when I'd get discouraged and wonder why He was allowing this to happen to me when I'd done my best to live a decent life and to stay true to my covenants with Him. At other times I'd imagine that I was being punished for something I'd done wrong, much like Job's friends tried to convince him that his tribulations were the result of some personal failing on his part. I was trying to comprehend the incomprehensible. I've found that when I'm discouraged I want to find a reason for things. But there was no good reason for the Germans to be doing this to us. The Allies were closing in on Germany, and yet the Germans persisted in marching us from one side of the country to the other. I suspected that they were simply following orders that had most likely been forgotten long ago by those who issued them. Fortunately, God did hear my prayers, and on more than one occasion I felt that He gave me strength beyond my natural abilities. Plus, the very act of praying gave my mind something positive to think about, and brought to mind the lessons from the scriptures I'd learned as a child in Sunday School, from young adult leaders, and from my mother. I felt safe when I thought of home, and it motivated me to keep going, hoping that somehow I might return there one day.

We didn't sing much anymore because it took too much effort. In fact, we didn't do anything we didn't have to. If a button came undone on someone's shirt they just left it that way because the effort of lifting your arms wasn't worth the trouble. We must have looked like a bunch of specters straggling through the muddy countryside. We'd started the march in the middle of one of the coldest winters on record, and now found ourselves trudging through the mud of a miserable early spring thaw. As much as I hated the cold, it was easier to walk on hard frozen ground than it was to struggle through the mud. It absorbed the energy of my footfall, forcing me to pull my legs up and out of the muck. I've never been so weak or exhausted in my life.

Eventually, as February yielded to March, I found that my earlier confidence of returning home to Afton and Randy began to fade. I contemplated just lying down and sleeping until all this misery was over. When I'd catch myself thinking that way, I'd say a prayer in my mind and ask for strength to keep going just one more day, one more day, and then one more day after that. I didn't get angry at the Germans anymore since it takes energy to get angry. I couldn't cry because we didn't get enough nourishment for that. I was so thin at this point that I could nearly wrap my belt around my waist twice, making it practically impossible to hold my threadbare pants up. I couldn't see what I looked like, but if it was anything like the others, it was a disturbing sight. Our beards were full, our clothes were filthy, our stomachs were sunken, and our countenance was haggard. It was a stark contrast to the well-nourished men I trained with.

Just when I thought I couldn't go any further, the Germans announced that we were going to camp for a few days in a large, open field surrounded by some pine trees. I found a coffee can and Lloyd,

Bob, and Roland made a hole in the can and found some wire to make a handle for it. We then looked around to see what ingredients we could find to make some hot soup. There were some roots and greens that had started to grow near a few of the more sheltered trees. The guards gave us permission to build a small fire, and pretty soon we had some steaming water. About that time one of the other prisoners came over and told us that he'd killed a cat, and he offered us some of the meat. It was quite greasy, but it felt wonderful to have the rich taste of the broth in our mouths, and the warmth of the fire and water brought a comfort we hadn't felt for a long time. On the second or third day at the camp a group of prisoners surrounded a horse and clubbed it to death. They offered me a nice-sized hunk of meat which I quickly cooked and devoured. I was so hungry and in such desperate need of nutrition that this meat may have saved my life. At the very least it kept a lot of us going for the next three or four days. The camp lasted for four days, and we had only the energy to lie around and sleep. It was just what the doctor would have ordered, if there had been a doctor to order it.

We'd covered a lot of territory by this point, and were coming closer and closer to the Allied lines. By my estimate based on the map I'd been keeping, we'd marched approximately 800 kilometers in the nearly three months we'd spent on the road. If I had interpreted our direction of travel correctly, we'd marched in an almost diagonal line from the northeastern corner of Germany to the southwestern border. If they kept us marching much longer we'd actually pass beyond the borders of Germany. Looking at the map, I couldn't understand what their intentions were.

In the evening we could see the big blasts from the heavy artillery light up the night sky as the Germans ferociously defended their homeland from the ever-increasing strength of the Allied onslaught. Sometimes we could even hear the sound of tanks rumbling in the distance as the Germans rushed reinforcements to the front lines. Allied aircraft flew over head almost constantly. The cold and hunger had taken its toll, and there had been a lot of casualties and deaths. It's impossible for me to estimate the number accurately, since our original group of 1000 was always spread out for miles along the road or trail. But I'd personally witnessed many men fall to the side of the road where they lay abandoned until long after we'd lost sight of them. I believe that most were left to die.

In a sense, we were all casualties. Our health was poor and we were nearing the end of our strength. Most of the time I was hopeful that the Allies would somehow liberate us, but there were times when I felt that we'd all die before they would. After all that we'd been through, I was almost to the point where it didn't really matter either way. One way or the other, the end was close.

CHAPTER 8

Another Miracle, Another Tragedy

As we continued to camp in the large clearing where we'd been allowed to rest for a few days, the guards started acting funny, like something was bothering them. I couldn't tell what they were planning or where they intended to move us. Most of the guys were just grateful to have time to rest, but I couldn't shake the uneasy feeling. My fears were confirmed when one of the friendlier guards came to me and whispered that we were going to move out the next day, and that shortly after that the SS were going to assume responsibility for guarding us. That turned my uneasiness into outright panic. I knew that we simply couldn't survive any more beatings from the SS.

Since everyone was lying around in small groups it was easy for me to approach Lloyd, Bob, and Roland to see what they thought about planning an escape. Bob caught his breath at the suggestion, and started outlining a number of reasons it would be too dangerous. If the Germans caught us they could shoot us, turn the dogs loose on us, or bring us back and take away our shoes, leaving us to walk in the remnants of our socks to wherever they were taking us. The last punishment was exactly what happened a few weeks earlier to one of the men from our barracks. He died of exposure while walking barefoot through the snow, and there was no reason to think we'd hold up any better.

Roland didn't have to say anything—he just pointed down to his pant legs where the Germans had painted the letters "PW" on each leg, as well as on the front and back of our shirt. This was to alert people that we were prisoners of war. These large, white letters were so obvious that they stood out even in the dark, truly making us "marked men."

"How," he asked, "could we ever pass through enemy territory undetected?"

I replied that we'd have to travel off the main roads at dusk or after nightfall. I thought we could make it without being discovered.

The biggest problem was our ability to travel given our emaciated condition. I had to admit that as weak as we were, it was really pretty crazy to even think of attempting an escape without reliable maps and food.

But as we continued talking, someone pointed out that if we didn't take the risk, we'd be at the mercy of the SS, who were capable of doing almost anything. Their hatred for the Allies would be at a fever pitch now that the Americans and English were closing in on Germany itself. In spite of the fact that Hitler kept circulating rumors that there was some dreadful weapon in the final stages of development that was powerful enough to destroy Germany's enemies, the only evidence we could see of the wars' progress was a helter-skelter deployment of forces that could only slow the advance of the Allies, but not stop it.

So, in spite of the danger, all four of us voted to attempt an escape. We put our heads together, without being too obvious, and came up with a general plan. First, we reviewed the terrain we'd covered on the last day of travel before pulling up for a rest, and came up with a secluded spot about a mile back where we would meet at midnight the next evening. Fortunately, all four of us remembered the place, so we were confident everyone could find it.

We also agreed that if someone didn't make it by midnight, we would assume he had been caught or changed his mind, and we'd head off without him.

A few days earlier I had traded three of the cigarettes I'd been saving (for an emergency) for a wristwatch from one the guards. A watch would aid in calculating both time and direction, since I could compare the position of the sun to the time of the day and get a better feel for the direction and distance traveled. It would also make it easier for us to choose the best times to travel to avoid detection.

The next afternoon around 1600 hours (4:00 P.M.) we passed the word up the line of prisoners that we were planning an escape, and asked if some of the other men would create a diversion by acting like they were having a big argument. It was risky, of course, to put the word out in case a guard overheard a whispered conversation, but it was the only practical way to slip out of the line unnoticed. In spite of having hundreds of men on the move, everyone was so quiet that any unusual sound could be detected.

The only way we would know if someone was going to help us out is if a fight actually broke out. For the next four or five minutes I walked forward with a deep feeling of dread, wondering if a guard was about to come racing back with his rifle pointed at me, or if we'd just continue to walk along in silence because none of the other prisoners were willing to risk punishment by starting a fight. I'm sure it was just my imagination, but I could actually hear the sound of my own breathing while I waited anxiously to see what was going to happen.

All of a sudden I heard some shouting up ahead. It sounded like angry voices, but I couldn't tell if it was in English, (which would mean the prisoners were creating our diversion) or just the yelling of a German guard who was angry at one of the prisoners. My heart was pounding so furiously in my ears that I had to focus all my attention on the sound. Sure enough, I heard a heated exchange in English, and saw some of the guards running up ahead to see what was going on. My heart pounded like crazy, and I decided that it was now or never.

I was the first one to drop out of line, and as I crawled into the bushes I was sure that someone would see me and report me. I crawled as fast as I could, trying to be quiet, praying all the time that the dogs wouldn't hear me and start barking. It was now a matter of life and death and I almost couldn't believe I was doing this. I didn't dare stand up to run (which is what I wanted to do), since my head would have shown above the brush. Instead, I half-crawled and half-stooped as I made my way through the forest undergrowth towards our pre-determined meeting spot. We'd chosen it because it was in a particularly dense part of the forest, with lots of bushes to hide in. I kept hoping that the others didn't chicken out or get caught. I was feeling really vulnerable.

I was so weak from the short rations we had been eating that I would go for a while and then have to sit down to catch my breath. Plus, I wanted to take periodic breaks so I could sit in absolute silence and listen for any indication that I was being followed or hear if there was some kind of a manhunt under way. Each time I paused, I was relieved to find there was nothing out of the ordinary—just the sounds of the forest, and an occasional report from one of the big guns far off in the distance. I'm not sure how long it took, but eventually I found my way to the small clearing where we had agreed to meet. I sat down and put my knees under my chin and prayed. I was so afraid to look around for fear I would see one of the German guards looking down at me.

I waited for what seemed longer than an eternity, and was growing increasingly alarmed waiting out in the forest all alone. Just then I heard the sound of rustling leaves. I slipped out of view, hoping that it was one of my friends rather than a German guard with his dog. My mouth was dry, and not just from the lack of food and water. I was crouched behind a large bush, trembling with anticipation, when I saw Lloyd Alburn stumble into the clearing. His red hair was a welcome sight. I crawled out of my hiding spot and stage-whispered, "Lloyd, I'm over here!" He was so thrilled to see me that he threw his arms around me and almost sobbed, "I was so scared, Joe, when I didn't see anyone in the clearing; I figured they'd caught you for sure."

I told him I knew exactly how he felt. It was bad enough to be on the run, but being alone was about more than I could take. I was as relieved as he was to have a companion.

A few minutes later Roland quietly stole into view, and we gave him a hug as well. The three of us sat down to rest while we waited for Bob to arrive. At first we expected him to show up in just a few minutes, since he would have traveled the same distance we did, but the minutes passed slowly with no sound or sign of him. By this time the light was fading into dusk, and with the loss of sunlight it started to get really cold. We all strained our ears to hear any sound of Bob or the Germans. I felt a little safer when total darkness snuffed out the last remnant of daylight, because at least no one could see us unless they came directly into our clearing. Of course the dogs were still a threat since they could probably sniff us out. I personally hoped that the guard who had befriended me would cover our disappearance, somehow, when they found we were missing in the evening roll call. Plus, with so many men dropping out of the march because of exhaustion, there was always the hope that the Germans would think we'd simply given up or passed out along the way.

Almost two more hours passed until we heard some noise in the brush. We huddled even closer together and remained absolutely silent. The noise stopped for a moment, and then we heard a timid voice say, "Roland, Joe, are you there?".

I was overjoyed that all four of us had made it safely, and I called out, "We're here, Bob, we're here. Where have you been?"

He choked up as he moved into the clearing. "I had to slip off the trail and wait for the group to march past me once the ruckus was over. It seemed like it took forever for them all to straggle by. When the coast was finally clear it was dusk and I had a hard time finding my way through the brush. I've spent the last few hours just trying to find you. I kept worrying that I was actually marching back towards the prison group, instead of toward the meeting spot."

Bob was so relieved to be with us he sort of slumped right where he stood. I can imagine that he'd used up all his energy racing back and forth in the darkness. We congratulated him on staying at it until he found us. I loved these guys. They had been my constant companions and best friends since I arrived in the prison camp. In the previous six months we'd spent virtually twenty-four hours a day together, and it just felt so much safer and happier with them around.

After giving Bob some time to catch his breath, the first thing we had to do was figure out which way to proceed. We decided to travel at night and lay low during the day to minimize the chance of being detected. That increased the risk, however, that without reference to the sun we'd get lost and actually work our way deeper into enemy territory. Just then we saw the distant sky brighten up as an artillery barrage was fired into the night sky. A light bulb turned on in my mind. Artillery was always fired from just behind the frontlines. All we had to do was move in the direction of the artillery blasts and we'd inevitably close the distance to the Allied lines. For us, these blasts became like the column of fire that went before the Israelites as they fled from Pharaoh in ancient Egypt.

After trying a number of different traveling positions, we decided that we would always travel towards the artillery, marching in single file about nine feet apart from each other. That way, if the enemy spotted one of us, the others would have a chance to duck behind cover to avoid detection. It was the responsibility of the lead position to determine the direction and pace of travel. In practice, it worked out that the leader would walk as quietly as possible for a while, then pause to make sure the others were still following. Sometimes the leader would look back and take a silent vote to see what we thought. The final rule was that we were to walk without talking to each other unless there was an emergency.

Occasionally, one of us had to signal a rest break because of the difficulty of walking through heavily forested brush, particularly in our starved condition. Moving through the darkness with only the faint illumination of the moon added to the labor because it was so easy to trip on a root or get slapped in the face with a branch.

Once daylight started to break we found a place to hide for the day. On that first morning we were totally exhausted, having spent nearly twenty-four hours awake. Thank heavens we'd had three days of rest in the large clearing before starting the current march. We each took turns acting as the watchman so the others could sleep. At first I didn't think I could fall asleep knowing that the Germans might be out looking for us, but the next thing I knew I was being startled awake by Roland to take my turn as watchman. We actually got some pretty decent sleep that first day.

On the second night when darkness started to fall, we were a little more relaxed about our escape. If the Germans had wanted to find us they could have used trained dogs to follow our trail, and it was highly unlikely that we could have outdistanced them given that the guards had plenty to eat compared to our meager rations. The very fact that we were still there was a pretty good sign that we'd made a clean break. I'm sure most of the guards assumed that we'd dropped in our tracks along the way, although the friendly guards who knew us best would be smart enough to doubt that all four of us, who stayed together constantly, would reach the end of our endurance at exactly the same time. I figured that they would just ignore our disappearance out of kindness, or so they didn't have to go out looking for us.

When it was dark enough that we felt safe traveling, the leader from the first night dropped to the second position and the person who had been in the fourth position at the rear assumed the role of leader for the coming day and night. By doing it this way we each took a turn at the leadership spot. If it turned out later that we had gone off course, we couldn't blame a single individual.

We didn't make a lot of progress the first two nights, just in case the guards had sent someone out to find us. We were also still trying to learn how to find our way in the darkness and to establish a routine. It was kind of tough for the person in the lead position to know if everyone else was still following, so we had to work out a series of hand signals to communicate up and down our four-person line.

Our biggest fear was that we'd accidentally wander back into the hands of the Germans. We all prayed for guidance, asking the Lord to help us find the best course of travel that would lead us to freedom, not further into enemy territory. As the nights wore on and we became more accustomed to our new mode of travel, we figured out that when we approached small towns it made sense to take a wide detour so as to not arouse the local dogs and alert the citizens. Sometimes it was pretty tough not to accidentally stumble into a hamlet, since every house was under a blackout order to keep all lights extinguished, or at least hidden behind impenetrable black curtains.

On the fourth night of our escape attempt we found a place where we thought we'd be safe in spite of the fact that there was no brush or branches to cover us. We were so exhausted that we just lay down together on our sides (the position where the blankets provided maximum coverage) and did our best to stay warm in the cold chill of morning. The blankets weren't long enough to fully cover us, so we'd pull them up around our neck and leave our feet out. We never undressed or took our shoes off, since we didn't know when we might have to jump up and make a run for it if someone was coming.

As the morning sun started to brighten our surroundings, we all froze in place at the sound of someone approaching. Whoever it was, he had managed to approach so closely that we didn't dare get up and make a run for it, so we just laid there as still as possible. Suddenly a German soldier came into view and spotted us immediately. He came striding over to us, yelling something in German. We lay still as if we were dead or asleep. He walked around us and kicked our feet, poking us with the muzzle of his rifle, talking all the time in German. Since none of us spoke German, we had no idea what he was saying. All we could do was pray silently and hope for the best. I imagine that he thought of shooting us just to make sure we were dead, but for some reason he didn't. He kicked us again, and then started hollering as loud as he could, probably for help. We still did not stir.

Finally he strode off through the bushes, calling out for help. As soon as he was out of sight, we got up and ran as fast as our weak legs could carry us. We didn't know what direction we were going, but we ran anyway. I don't know how far we ran, but we were all breathless by the time Lloyd called out that he couldn't go any farther without some rest. We tried to get him to keep going, and he tried for a little ways, but he almost passed out on us. Even though we were terrified of being caught, we had made a pact to stick together. We quickly found some thick bushes and trees, and climbed in and lay there on our bellies where we could see if anybody approached. From this vantage point we could see that we had actually been paralleling a road that was used by the German soldiers on their way to and from the front lines. It was fortunate that none of them had heard or seen us. Given that there was at least one soldier that knew we were out there, with dozens of others nearby, we decided to lay low right where we were until it was safe to sneak further away from the road and the soldiers.

When it seemed safe to move, we scurried away from the road and traveled in a crouching position until we came in sight of a farm. It was pretty quiet, and by now it was full daylight, so we hid in some bushes and tried to sleep. After our scare, it was hard to relax enough to sleep, but we managed to get at least a few hours of rest. As it grew late in the afternoon we decided that someone had to sneak over to the barn to see if there was any food. Out on our own we hadn't found any food to replace the boiled potatoes that had kept us going as prisoners. After four nights without any food we were famished, and our energy was fading quickly. We drew lots to see who would crawl to the barn, and, as luck would have it, the lot fell to me. We were hidden in a thick grove of pine trees, but the barn sat in the middle of a large, snow-covered clearing.

To improve my chances of getting there without being spotted I waited until twilight. It was still a bit lighter than I would've liked, but if I waited any longer the moon and stars would make it even worse. Mustering all my courage and strength, I slowly and quietly slipped across the barnyard and felt my way to the door. It was closed and did not immediately yield to the pressure I applied. I don't know if it was stuck, or if I was just too weak to apply much force, but try as I might, I couldn't get it to budge. Having come this far, I wasn't about to go back empty handed, so I looked around until I found a two-by-four board, which I wedged into a small opening that allowed me to pry the door open. It made a creaking sound and I winced for fear someone in the farmhouse would hear it. I slipped quickly inside and stood with my back to the wall just inside the door. I stayed absolutely silent, except for the noise of my heart pounding inside my chest. I strained to hear if anyone was coming but heard nothing.

After a while I let myself relax and catch my breath. By this time, everything we did was an effort and it seemed like we were always winded. After calming down I gave my eyes time to adjust to the dim light and then started to explore the interior of the barn. I didn't have a lantern, but there were enough holes in the walls letting in shafts of light from the setting sun that I could see the interior of the barn pretty well. Before long I found a treasure that at that particular moment was worth more to me than a wheelbarrow full of gold. Off in a corner I stumbled onto a pile of kohlrabis, which are a cross between a turnip and rutabaga, with a tough exterior and a stringy yellow flesh inside. I was so excited because this was something we could eat without having to cook, and they would be relatively easy to carry. I gathered as many as I could in my arms, inched my way back to the door, and pushed it open with my foot. As I stepped outside into the afternoon gloom I was startled to see a light come on inside the house. I immediately stepped back inside the barn and dropped to the floor. I lay perfectly still as I heard someone approach the outside of the barn. I prayed and prayed that once again I could somehow be invisible, and that I wouldn't get caught. I heard the footsteps walk all around the barn and just when I thought the door would open, I heard the footsteps turn and head back to the house.

I waited a long time before finally getting the courage to go back to the entrance. I was afraid that they might be waiting just outside the door to clobber me on the head, so I pushed it open very gently with my foot. I didn't hear anything, so I stuck my head outside and looked in the direction of the house. The light went out, so I sneaked out into the barnyard and quietly crossed the open ground back to where the other three were waiting. They had seen the whole thing and were so happy that I'd made it without being caught. They were ecstatic to see all the kohlrabis, and we settled back to eat for the next few hours before starting out again. The kohlrabis were about as hard as a rock and the best you could do was to bite a chunk out with your teeth and chew the fibrous flesh until you'd extracted all the juice you could, then spit out the pulp. They tasted wonderful, and for the first time in months we were able to savor food in our mouth without fear of not being able to take another bite. To me, the kohlrabis were like manna from heaven, and I ate until the pain in my stomach started to ease.

It's amazing how quickly the food gave a boost to both my body and my attitude. It was like giving water to a wilting flower. Suddenly I had the ability to think more clearly, and my legs actually felt stronger than they had in days. It was a great feast in the middle of our wilderness.

After the meal we tried to catch an hour's sleep before setting out into the darkness. Our plan to walk at night and sleep during the day didn't work out very well because our anxiety that we'd be discovered made it almost impossible to sleep. In addition to having little food and suffering from the cold temperatures, we were tired most of the time. But in spite of that, we concluded that we must be making some progress, since the flash of the heavy artillery was getting noticeably closer, and we could feel the concussions reverberate through the cold night air.

Three nights after finding the kohlrabis we were walking single file through the brush when we came to the outskirts of a very small village. It looked like one of the places we'd marched through while under guard. In their attempt to keep from falling into the hands of the Allies, our German guards had actually marched us past the closest approach, so we were now backtracking over ground we'd already covered while under guard. I think it was Lloyd who said that he thought he remembered passing by some apple orchards on the other end of this town, if this was the place he thought it was. We speculated that there might be some frozen apples lying on the ground, or maybe even some that hadn't fallen from the tree. The thought of eating fruit was a powerful temptation, so we decided to violate our own rule of always walking out and around a town, and to instead proceed carefully and quietly through the town. The forest was so thick in this area that it would have been a lot of work to go out and around, and since there were only fifteen or twenty houses it didn't seem worth the bother. There was no light anywhere since everyone used their blackout curtains on the windows, and it was late enough that we figured most everyone would be asleep anyway. The only danger was disturbing any dogs that might be about, but with all the noise of the war they tended to bark anyway, so we hoped people wouldn't pay any attention if they started barking at us.

The place was so small that there was only one road to walk on, so we cautiously proceeded down the single cobblestone lane through the center of the town to reach the other side. On this particular night Roland was in the lead, followed by Bob, Lloyd, and then me in the Tail End Charlie position. My natural inclination would be to hug the side of the road to stay out of sight, but Roland started straight down the middle of the road. At first I couldn't figure out his reasoning, but then realized that going down the middle of the lane lessened the chance that one of us would accidentally brush up against a house and disturb the occupants. We crept along slowly and deliberately, hardly making a sound, maintaining about ten feet between each member of our team. Roland was a great leader at times like this because he never got excited or panicked.

By the time we reached the middle of the town we were relieved that no dogs had started barking, and it looked like we were going to make it. Suddenly I was startled by a voice in the darkness. As I instinctively turned to look, a door opened from a house on my left. The light from inside shone on me and it was such an unexpected contrast from the darkness that it temporarily blinded me. I stood there like a deer caught in the headlights of an oncoming car, unable to move. Suddenly a German soldier came striding out of the house straight for me, followed by a woman. Fortunately the field of light was restricted enough so they could only see me, giving my three partners a chance to take cover. As the soldier got closer, his shadow shielded my eyes enough for me to see a huge German tank parked next to the house. I could see the excited look in his eyes. I stood there transfixed, unable to move or even make a sound. I didn't know whether to run, put my hands up, or fall to my knees and beg for mercy, so I just stood there. When he reached me he shouted something unintelligible in German. Before I could think of what to do, I was startled to hear myself respond with a calm, confident German phrase that was obviously appropriate to what he'd asked me. He then replied to whatever I'd said with an almost cheerful, "Ya, Ya, Ya!" Then he put his arm around the woman, turned his back on me, and went back into the house and closed the door. I was so astonished and frightened that I simply stood there with my mouth open. My buddies had seen and heard the whole thing, and when I didn't move, they came out and grabbed me and pulled me behind a nearby outbuilding where we could hide.

The whole encounter took only a few seconds. The first thing my buddies asked was, "What on earth did he say to you, and what did you say when you talked back to him?" I told them that I had no idea what either he or I said, since I couldn't speak German. I knew that I didn't use any of the few German words that I'd learned in POW camp, like "Hello," "Yes, sir," or "No, sir." Even if I had, my accent would have been so terrible that a German would have recognized me as a foreigner immediately. Yet whatever I said had satisfied him. All of us stood there marveling in disbelief at what had just happened.

Considering that I was standing fully in plain sight of this soldier with my straggly beard, tattered clothes, no coat, and bright white letters painted on my trousers and shirt indicating that I was a P.O.W., it was just impossible that he didn't recognize me as an escaped prisoner. Instead of shooting me or calling for help, though, he looked straight at me, spoke to me in his native language, listened to my response in a foreign language that I had never spoken before, and he accepted my answer as legitimate. Even if the guard hadn't figured it out, there was the woman who also stared at me and heard the words that passed between us. Why didn't either of them figure out what was going on?

As all of this settled in my mind, I felt a burning in my heart that told me that I had been blessed once again, and that the Holy Ghost had interpreted what the German had said to me and put the appropriate words in my mouth to respond. I'd been blessed with the gift of tongues. I don't know what those two Germans saw, but obviously they didn't see the letters on my clothing—though they should have stood out like a neon sign in the bright light that shone through the door. The Spirit may have also changed what they saw. I think in some way my appearance had been transformed so they did not recognize me.

I've heard it said that for something to be a miracle there can be no logical or earthly way to explain it. If that's true, then I was clearly the beneficiary of a miracle, and it thrilled me to know that God was still watching out for me and that He cared for me. Here in the middle of Germany, with millions of lives in turmoil, He had time to remember me and provide help in a desperate moment. My heart was filled with joy and appreciation, and I immediately testified to the others that it was Heavenly Father who protected and saved us just then. There was silence for a while as we each thought about it. Then we all agreed that it had to be a miracle. We said a silent prayer of thanks, and even though we should have been anxious to get out of there, everyone stood still for a few a minutes to bask in the glow of the warm feeling that surrounded us.

Unfortunately, moments like that don't last very long, and soon the urgency of our situation forced us to continue our journey through town. When we reached the other side of town there was indeed a small apple orchard, but there were only a couple of frozen apples left by the trees, and about half of each apple was rotten. By the time we cut them down to the edible portion there wasn't a lot to go around. Still, we were grateful for any food we could get. As escapees on the run we couldn't ask anyone for help, so we took advantage of whatever nourishment presented itself.

I remember when we got out into the open beyond the town, where it was safe to speak openly, we talked about how spoiled we'd been before the war, throwing out perfectly good food. Even in the darkest days of the Depression we'd never been hungry like this. We vowed that if we got out of this alive, we'd eat all the food that was put before us without complaint.

By the end of our first week on the lam we knew we were getting closer to the front lines. Allied aircraft flew overhead nearly all hours of the day, and at night we heard the rumble of tanks, the concussion of heavy artillery, and sometimes even machine gun fire. We had to be a lot more careful to avoid retreating German soldiers.

By this point we had our routine down pretty well, and were getting pretty self-assured in our ability to avoid detection by the retreating German troops. In order to keep our sense of direction we traveled as close to the highways as we dared, but always far enough out of sight to avoid detection. We didn't speak or even whisper when there was any sign of the enemy, and mostly used signs and gestures to communicate with each other. Most days were spent lying on our stomachs in the snow or mud so we didn't offer anyone a visible target.

One of the most glorious sights in my life was to watch a company of SS troops move by in full retreat one afternoon. As mean and cruel as they'd been to us, it made me want to stand up and shout to the world that the Americans had beaten them. I'd have loved the chance to rub their noses in that truth, but of course we stayed well hidden, knowing full well that they would love to shoot four miserable-looking American prisoners of war. That night we crept back out onto the road and continued working our way forward in the opposite direction of the retreat. It was nerve-racking, listening for any sound from any direction, but we felt we had to keep moving forward to shorten the distance to friendly lines.

On the ninth night of our escape we hid in the bushes because there was a massive movement of infantry and tanks from the front lines. It was noisy and slightly unnerving to lie on the ground as those lumbering giants moved through the thick underbrush with their treads groaning to support the massive burden of steel, their diesel engines belching foul-smelling fumes. The ground shook beneath us whenever a tank passed nearby, and I would always hold my breath, hoping that we'd found a decent place to hide so that a tank wouldn't crush us to death. The closest one ever got was fifteen or twenty feet away.

Watching the troops, tanks, and artillery pull back was like having a front row seat at a sporting event, and we were watching the losing team retrenching, perhaps to surrender, perhaps to launch another counter-attack. It was such an odd feeling to be a silent observer, hidden from view, but vitally interested in the outcome of the conflict.

All this activity forced us to spend the following day and night in hiding. When possible we'd hide just inside the brush at the base of a row of trees. From here we could look out on the open space to where the main German forces were moving down the forest roads. We favored this approach over hiding further inside the line of trees since it gave us the chance to see in advance any guard patrols that might be moving towards our position.

The troop movement was so general that there was really no place we could move through without being detected. For the moment, we had to stay put and wait for the Germans to retreat past our position. We took advantage of the interlude to make a plan for crossing into friendly territory. Not too far distant from our present position we could see a large open field near a farmhouse and barn. Someone suggested that if we could go to the barn and find a shovel we could dig a foxhole in the middle of the field and cover ourselves while it was still dark, then wait for the Allied troops to overrun our position. That way we wouldn't have to approach our troops from the enemy side where they could easily mistake us for the enemy. After considering a number of different alternatives, we decided that this was our best hope.

That night we crept across the field to the barn, where luck provided the shovel we'd hoped for. Crawling back out to the middle of the field we took turns digging. It was pretty tough work since the ground in mid-March was still a bit frozen. The field had been created by cutting out a stand of thick pine trees, which left numerous roots and small brush to cut through. With only the kohlrabis and apples to nourish us in the past ten days we had little strength left for physical labor. We made little progress in digging the hole at first, and I became anxious that we were too exposed in the open field to be spending so much time in an upright position. But once we'd broken through the frozen crust of the ground the digging was easier and the outlines of a hole large enough to conceal us started to appear. We were so tired, but the urgency of our situation gave us the motivation to make our poor muscles do the required work.

The task of digging occupied most of the night. Finally we had a shallow hole, probably two feet deep, that was just big enough for us to lie down in pairs, with our heads in the center, and our feet to each end. That way we could easily talk to each other if the need arose.

The next step was to go back to the barn to get some planks that we pulled over top of the hole, then camouflaged it with some pine boughs and brush from the nearby woods. Just as daylight approached, we climbed inside, pulled the cover over our heads, and lay down to wait. The hole was so small that we were quite snug up against each other, with our blankets to keep us warm.

Waiting was boring and anxious. Occasionally we'd peek out to watch the German troop withdrawal. On a couple of occasions the German troops came so close to our hole that we could hear them speaking to each other. Their voices sounded frantic and frightened. For us, it was nerve-racking to wonder if they'd stumble on our position and discover the crude camouflage that covered our hiding place.

After two days and nights in our underground shelter the ground began to rumble, and we looked out to see German tanks coming straight for us. This was it! The tanks would be the last to leave the battlefield, so the end was near. As the first tank approached, the ground started shaking and dust fell in from the boards above. Lloyd let out a startled cry, then quickly stifled it. With all the noise of the tank I doubt that anyone could have heard him, but we were so highly practiced at suppressing all sounds that his was a natural reaction. I peeked out of the hole and saw that the whole field was filled with tanks covering the withdrawal of the infantry. I felt my heart pounding in my ears as the ground trembled. We couldn't help but wonder if the retreating infantry troops would spot our position and stop to check it out, or whether their tanks would crush us as they passed overhead.

We soon got an answer to our question. The ground trembled furiously as a German Panzer tank rumbled directly over the top of our foxhole. The noise so terrifying that we covered our eyes and ears as best we could, while trying hard not to choke on all the dust that was falling in on us. We could have shouted at the top of our lungs and no one would have heard us. I prayed fervently that the hole wouldn't cave in and bury us alive. We could only hope that the treads of the tank would straddle our hole. I looked up to see the treads roll directly over the center of the hole. Fortunately, the ground was frozen hard enough that the sides didn't collapse under the weight.

Then it was over. The relief was almost instantaneous as the noise subsided, the ground stopped rumbling, and the dirt started to settle. We suffered no ill effects other than the dust and debris that fell in on us.

We heard several other German tanks pass some distance away, and then there was total silence. No German voices, no sound of engines, not even any artillery fire. It was eerie, given the intensity of the experience that we'd been through just an hour earlier. Roland reached up, pushed one of the boards to the side, and stuck his head up to see what was out there.

"Nothing," he reported. "There's not a thing moving out here at all."

He pulled the board back into place, making sure to arrange the camouflage to cover it, then laid back down in the hole. It was so quiet that we didn't dare talk, even though it seemed certain that all the Germans were gone.

Although we'd been laying there for more than forty-eight hours, it was only now that I started to feel claustrophobic. My body hurt from lying still so long, and I just couldn't stand the thought of having another tank pass overhead. Just as I was about to say something, we heard the approach of another tank in the distance. One of us stuck his head up just far enough to see the new tank. Painted on the front was a big white star, indicating that it was an Allied tank! Wow! Talk about jubilation. We wanted to climb out right on the spot and run for their protection. I think it was Roland who cautioned that we should probably stay down for a while, just in case the Germans had captured the tank and staffed it with their own people. Reluctantly we allowed this new formation of tanks to roll by our position before we concluded that they were indeed Americans, and that it was safe to give ourselves up.

During a lull in the advance we used our last remaining strength to push the planking aside, and stood in the foxhole with our heads above ground. After nearly two weeks of living like nocturnal creatures, it was pretty frightening to stand fully exposed in broad daylight. It felt like we stood there for a couple of hours, although it was undoubtedly less than half an hour. Off in the distance we heard the ominous rumble of a tank, and in a few moments the ground started to shake. A huge tank loomed into sight, headed straight for us. It felt like we were standing in the middle of the railroad tracks with a locomotive approaching. There was no need to whisper now, so we yelled to each other, "What if it's a mistake and it turns out to be the Germans?" We figured our luck couldn't be that bad—we'd gone through too much, and it just couldn't be anybody but the Allies. As the tank drew closer we saw a white star on the front, indicating that it was American, so we scrambled out of the foxhole and started waving our arms and hollering for them to stop and rescue us. It was so exciting my heart pounded furiously in my chest.

The tank ground to a stop. Then its huge gun swung in a wide arc until it pointed directly at us. Someone yelled, "Oh, my gosh, they're going to shoot us!" Suddenly my legs felt like jelly and I almost fell to the ground. Then we heard a metallic sound as the upper hatch swung open and fell against the body of the tank with a clunking sound. To my surprise, four British soldiers emerged with pistols aimed directly at us. They shouted "Put your arms up in the air!"

After raising our arms as high as we could, we didn't know what to do next: should we say something and run the risk of getting shot on the spot, or wait until they took some kind of action? It was a silent, unanimous decision to wait. They could see the large "prisoner of war" letters painted on our clothes, so we couldn't understand their reason for treating us this way. Finally their officer shouted for us to identify ourselves. It was disorienting to hear a strong British accent. We were all so weak from malnutrition that I struggled to make out what he was asking. One of the guys called back that we were American airmen who had escaped from a prisoner of war camp. Even then they didn't put their guns down. The officer called back that it had been reported by some tank companies that they had come across men dressed like Allied prisoners of war, who in reality were armed Germans masquerading as POWs. All of a sudden we could see why they were being so hesitant to help us. I called out to them with as strong a voice as I could, "Listen to how well we speak English!"

They replied that some of the German saboteurs had spoken English as good or better than we did, (or perhaps with a better British accent). What to do next? I called back to him, "Ask us anything you want about America."

One of their men shouted back "What kind of sports do you like?"

"Baseball and football!"

"Tell me more about baseball, like who was in last year's World Series in America?"

"The last World Series that I know anything about was in 1943, and the New York Yankees beat the St. Louis Cardinals."

I was about to say more when he interrupted and said, "Tell me some of the players' names."

I was on solid ground now. I knew many of them. "Frankie Crossetti, Charlie "King Kong" Keller, and Bill Dickey."

He stopped me again and asked if I knew any of the pitchers.

"Spud Chandler!" I shouted, sounding just as confident as I could with guns aimed at my forehead.

With that he said, "Okay, come closer, but keep your hands in the air!"

I nearly passed out with relief, and I heard the others exhale.

When we got close enough for them to search us they found that we were unarmed. The officer said, "Okay, I guess you guys are Americans."

I was so excited I could have hugged and kissed them, but for some reason they didn't want to stand too close to us. It had been so long since I'd had any clean clothing that I didn't even stop to think what we must have looked and smelled like. Still, I was thrilled that we'd managed to surrender to a British soldier who was also a Yankee fan. It just didn't get any better than that.

For the first time since arriving in the combat zone in North Africa I felt safe. I'm sure there was danger there, but right then we were in the hands of friends and out of the Germans' reach. Standing next to that massive tank was like being sheltered by a well-armed fortress. The four of us sunk to the ground, our legs too weak to hold us upright any longer. The British commander radioed back for assistance from the medical corps. The tank crew took a break and chatted with us while we waited for a truck to take us to a medical tent just behind the front line. It was encouraging to hear that the Allies were closing on Berlin. When asked where we'd been taken prisoner, they were astonished that it was up on the Polish border. They asked how we got this far south and west, almost on the direct opposite side of the country. We told them about our enforced winter march across the hills and plains of central Germany, and they confirmed my earlier estimate that we'd traveled more than eight hundred kilometers. Fortunately, we were far enough north to avoid the mountainous areas of south-central Germany that would have made the task even more arduous. As we talked about the distance covered it seemed incredible even to us that we had been able to travel that far on foot, in winter, and in our condition.

When our transport arrived we thanked our British "captors" with tears of joy. They wished us good luck and rumbled off to pursue the retreating Germans, and hopefully to liberate other people like us. The British medics helped us into the back of their ambulance and drove us to their headquarters.

When the truck pulled to a stop we tried to stand up and lower ourselves out of the back, but our arms and legs were so weak that we practically fell out. Medics rushed over and helped us walk into a nearby tent, where they propped us up on a bench. An English officer sat next to me and asked my name, rank, and serial number. It felt a lot better to give this information to him than it did to my German captors almost nine months earlier.

"Joseph Banks, 39910833, Staff Sergeant, U.S. Army Air Corp," I replied with a shaky voice. I then reached under my shirt and took off both sets of dog tags, my American ones and the set issued to me by the Germans.

When he saw the German dog tags, he asked me in a quieter voice, "How do you feel, sergeant? Are you okay?"

I told him that I was overjoyed to be rescued, but that we were all very hungry and weak. I asked if we could we have some food. He immediately got up and called out an order for some food. They brought me a hard-boiled egg and a piece of cheese. I was so famished I would have swallowed it all whole, but they cautioned me to eat very slowly and chew the food thoroughly before swallowing it. They carefully watched the four of us and would reach out and take the food away if anyone tried to gulp it down. That egg and cheese tasted better than anything I had eaten in my life. It had been so long since I'd had any kind of variety to the food I ate. It was lucky they didn't offer more, since I would have probably eaten as much as they would let me.

I thought this new food would provide some relief to the empty feeling in my stomach, but instead it settled into a lump and caused immediate cramping. A doctor came in and I told him that my stomach hurt from the food; I couldn't understand why. He explained that it was a natural reaction when people haven't had very much to eat. I told him that I hadn't had anything to eat (except a few kohlrabis) for nearly two weeks.

At this point each of my friends was assigned to an individual doctor, and we were separated from one another. My assigned doctor took out a pad of paper and a pencil and started asking questions. The first was "How long ago did you escape?"

I explained about our camp near Poland and how more than a thousand of us had marched around eight hundred kilometers to the western border of Germany.

He then asked, "What happened to the other prisoners?"

I told him about the friendly German guard warning us about the SS, which prompted the four of us to escape. I added that I was very concerned for the other prisoners and pleaded with him to try to get help to them as soon as possible. I did my best to identify our direction of travel, but it was difficult to do since we had traveled mostly at night, using only the blasts of the artillery as our guide to reach the frontlines. He wrote all this down, went out and gave it to someone, then came back to ask a few more questions about our medical condition.

He was very interested in the quantity and type of food we'd had during the past six months, whether we had dysentery, and if there were any wounds that hadn't fully healed, etc. I think he wanted to ask more questions about the other prisoners in our group, but unfortunately I just didn't have the strength to tell him what he wanted. He stopped the questioning when he could see that I was shaking, sweating, and freezing all at the same time. Two other doctors came in and took me to an examination room to check me out. When I stepped off the scale I was stunned to hear them say, "97 lbs." At five foot, seven and a half inches tall, I'd weighed 140 lbs. before the war. I had lost one-third of my body mass.

Once the doctors determined that I was medically stable enough to bear the strain of more tests, they asked permission to take some x-rays. I hadn't undressed for months and when I took off my clothes I was shocked to see that I was just a bunch of coarse skin drawn over some bones, with no fat at all. My legs were shriveled, but rock hard from the eight hundred kilometer walk. I looked and felt like a specter, not quite human in appearance. When the doctors returned a few minutes later with the developed x-rays they told me that my stomach was the size of a tangerine, and that they couldn't find all of my large intestine. I told them that it was no wonder, given the way I'd been going to the bathroom from dysentery—at least twenty to twenty-five attempted bowel movements per day and no urinating. On our pathetic diet of half a potato and the few kohlrabis we'd eaten on the escape, there was nothing for my stomach to process.

Both doctors were amazed that we'd even survived. They warned me that I must eat only the small amounts of food they planned to give me for a while, for anything more would surely overwhelm my digestive system and kill me. This was scary to hear, and I wasn't emotionally prepared for this type of news. It was hard to accept that I couldn't immediately enjoy the fruits of freedom. For six months the only thing that had sustained me were my dreams of getting rescued and then going home to the states to resume my life. Now the doctors were telling me that my health was precarious and that I would have to go through a lengthy, supervised recovery. It was almost as if the Germans still held me prisoner. Yet in spite of the disappointment it was wonderful to be with friendly people who were concerned about me and were trying to help. We had been treated with indifference or contempt for so long that it was comforting to hear a pleasant and concerned sound in people's voices.

I was so exhausted that the doctors led me to a cot where I could lie down and rest. I didn't walk very far on my own before my legs gave out and I fell to the ground. It took so much energy to get up. The strong hands of the doctors reached down and helped me up and into bed. While it was embarrassing to be a burden, I needed help to do almost anything.

On the second or third day after our rescue, I asked one of the officers if they'd found the rest of the prisoners in our group and liberated them. The question must have caught him off guard because his face clouded up and he grew serious. He then asked me to sit down. He sort of choked up as he told me of his difficulty in relating this, but reports had been received that the British had come upon the site of a burned-out barn, filled with the bones and ashes of Allied prisoners. Apparently the Germans had boarded the prisoners in the barn one night, locked the doors, then set it on fire. When the desperate prisoners broke the door down to escape the fire, the SS machine-gunned them down as they emerged from the burning building. I was stunned. I asked him if anyone had escaped, and he replied that as of the last report, no survivors had been found.

I was sick to my stomach at this news. While Lloyd, Bob, and Roland were my best friends in the camp, I knew dozens of the others. The thought that they had all been murdered was overwhelming and I started shaking when I heard it. I could picture it all happening in my mind, and the image was horrifying. After the doctor left I said a fervent prayer that the report was in error, and that somehow God had helped my former comrades. Part of me didn't want to believe it had even happened. Or, at the very least, that it wasn't my group. But knowing how the SS had treated us along the way, I had the dreadful feeling that this report was accurate. In spite of everything the Germans had done to us, it was unbelievable to think that they might actually commit an atrocity of this magnitude. It didn't make sense that the Germans had made those men walk for three months through the hellish winter of 1945, only to destroy them when liberation was within their grasp. I've wondered what really happened to those who didn't escape with us, but I've never heard from any of them or been able to find any solid information about their fate. If the report of their massacre was true, may their names be added to the list of those who lost their lives in the battle for freedom.

I once again found myself saying a prayer of thanks to God for preserving my life. I felt so sorry for the others and their families back home, and I recognized that it was only through God's help that I'd come this far. I was grateful to the German prison guard who had warned me that the SS would be taking over. He was really the one who saved our lives, because it was his warning that motivated us to risk our lives in an escape attempt. I don't know why he did it, other than the fact that I'd befriended him and shown him some respect along the way.

On the fourth day after our rescue I was reunited with my companions. It was great to see them again. Their health had improved noticeably, even after a few days. The British told us that they were going to fly us to Brussels, Belgium, for transfer to a fully equipped hospital that could better take care of our medical needs. I asked if the aircraft was provided with parachutes for the passengers, and was dismayed to hear them say no, they didn't do that on a troop transport. I said I didn't want to fly because I'd been shot out of the air once, and didn't want to risk it happening again. They told me I didn't really have a choice since they were so poorly equipped to care for us. They didn't even have any new clothes to offer us. In true military fashion we accepted our fate and boarded a large military transport. We huddled close to each other through the whole flight. At first my anxiety level was high, but before the flight was over I'd calmed down a lot and actually enjoyed the sensation of flying again. It helped to know that we were in secure air space where there would be no Triple A to fly through, no enemy fighters trying to shoot us from the sky.

As soon as the aircraft landed in Brussels an ambulance took us to a large hospital where they took us directly to a locker room. The orderlies told us to take off our clothes so we could have a hot shower. I hadn't bathed for nine months. I stripped down and held my clothes out for them. They took the clothes with a stick and didn't touch them. Our clothing, like our skin, was infested with lice and bedbugs. Our clothing was put in sacks and taken out to be burned.

Meanwhile, I climbed under the nozzle of the hot water and felt like I'd died and gone to heaven. It was so wonderful to lather up, clean myself, and let the water soak into my aching muscles and bones. I probably could have stayed in the shower for a couple of years, but after a while the attendants told us to turn them off so they could dust us with a white powder to kill any lice that hadn't been washed away. We closed our eyes and held our arms out while they sprayed the powder all over our bodies and hair until we looked like white statues. We then turned the showers back on and washed the powder off. They also provided a special disinfectant shampoo for our hair. I felt much better after the shower. I sat on a bench, savoring the unfamiliar sensation of being clean. My skin felt funny to the touch from the effects of being malnourished, but at least it was clean.

I was surprised when they handed me a new set of English uniforms that were clean and well pressed. I asked if they didn't have a U.S.A. Air Force uniform, but they sniffed that they only had English clothing, so this would have to do. I proudly donned new, long wool pants, high stockings, and a wool shirt that drowned me in size. I was also fit with a set of beautiful English leather shoes that had steel toes and metal taps that clicked when I walked down the hall. Life just kept getting better.

The ward they assigned us to included other patients who were suffering from the same sorts of ailments we were, and so we had a lot of stories to share with one another. Some of the men were quite talkative, while others were almost completely withdrawn and emotionally isolated. It was so different than basic training, where the rooms had been filled with healthy young men anxious to get into the action. Now we were a bunch of skeletons with a little skin, hardly able to keep any food or liquid down. It was almost amusing to watch us stagger and down the corridors. Our bony legs could barely support the weight of our own body as we staggered back and forth.

During the first few days in the hospital they continued to monitor our condition and feed us sparingly. I always wanted to eat more, but they kept the portions small and bland. We ate mostly cold foods since those were the easiest for the digestive system to handle.

I still suffered from dysentery, and now that I had some food to digest I was grateful there were real toilets to use. Some people objected to the smell of a hospital, but after what I'd been through it was wonderful to smell antiseptics and disinfectants, and to be able to care for my body in a clean environment.

The medical examiners continued to take copious notes about our experiences and conditions, in part, I think, to create a reference point for future treatment, and also to document the treatment we'd received at the hands of the Germans. While I had no idea what else had gone on in Germany during the war, it was clear that our doctors were disgusted by our poor condition and wanted to record the hard evidence in our medical records.

On the third day we were feeling so well we wanted to get outside and enjoy some fresh air. We asked if we could have a pass to go into the city. The doctors agreed, but only if we promised to not eat or drink anything at all—particularly liquor. They threatened that if we disobeyed orders we could get ourselves in real medical trouble. Everyone promised. As soon as we got out of sight of the orderlies, however, two of the men headed straight for a tavern to get some booze. We tried to stop them, but they were dead set on tasting some alcohol again. They ordered some Italian liquor, which they said was something like vodka. They started guzzling it down and in about five to ten minutes they both started to throw up everything in their stomachs. In just a few moments they were vomiting blood and lay moaning and writhing on the ground in agony. We tried to help, but there was nothing we could do. They died right there on the street in front of us. The ambulance came from the hospital, and the orderlies loaded them on stretchers and ordered us to get in. That was the end of our privileges, and we spent the rest of our time in Brussels under medical guard in the hospital. This experience scared all of us by showing just how fragile our health was, and how easily we could lose our life if we didn't follow instructions.

After about a week at this hospital they gave us the welcome news that we were flying to an American Air Force base in "Lucky Strike," France, where we'd be transferred to a long-range transport for a flight back to America. We were so excited we could hardly sleep that night. The flight to France was short and uneventful. The following morning Lloyd, Roland, and Bob received their orders to ship out, but one of the medical officers came up to me and said, "I'm sorry, but your health is just too fragile to leave you unattended for that long, so you're going to have to go home by hospital ship." I was sorely disappointed because I was so anxious to get home. But after seeing how easily a person in my condition could get into trouble, I decided that the medical staff knew what was best for me.

When the time came for my three companions to leave I gave them each a big hug and told them how much I appreciated their friendship. They did their best to cheer me up and to wish me well in my recovery. I had a huge lump in my throat and wanted to cry as they boarded the aircraft. After spending nine awful months with them they had become my best friends, and now I was being left behind. It was a terribly lonely feeling.

Yet I knew with all my heart that God had preserved my life on many occasions, and it comforted me to think that His spirit was with me now. He must have had something in mind for my life. I just needed to find out what it was.

CHAPTER 9

Recuperation and Return to Civilian Life

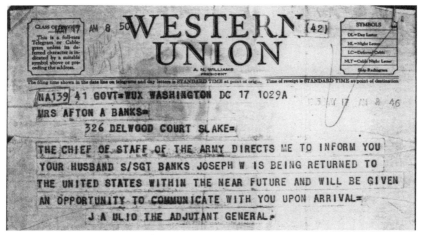

Great news for the folks at home. May 17, 1945.

After watching Lloyd, Roland, and Bob board the aircraft for their return to the United States, I had several hours to wait before being transferred to the hospital ship. A feeling of loneliness swept over me as I thought about them. I wanted to get up and walk around, but I just didn't have the strength to move around for any length of time. I was pretty discouraged by the time I was taken to a pier to board a large white ship with huge red crosses painted on it. Fortunately, the activity of checking in and finding my way to the correct hospital ward gave me something to do, which cheered me up a bit.

Once on board I was issued a pair of pajamas, a robe, and slippers, and told to go to bed, which is where I stayed for most of the duration of the trip. When we pulled into port in England to pick up some other wounded Americans, the most I could do was stand at the rail and look out on that great country that had stood with us throughout the war. I felt deep appreciation for the kindness with which the British medical staff had treated me.

The first few days of the crossing to New York were uneventful. The staff continued to monitor my food and experiment with diets that would alleviate my dysentery. I was able to hold more and more down, but I still wasn't gaining weight very well and I continued to suffer from stomach cramps, frequently visiting the bathroom.

Before the war I would have been curious to learn more about this great ship, but now I was still too weak to really care. I did find myself pondering about my experiences a lot, and it amazed me to think that in the past two years I'd been to Africa, Italy, the Isle of Capri, Germany, Belgium, France, and even had a passing glance at England. Before the war my only real travel had been to Washington, D.C., to a national Boy Scout Jamboree. Now I'd traveled on three continents. I knew I was fortunate to have survived the many ordeals that we passed through, and I was happy to be going home, but I still brooded about the things I'd seen. My thoughts were particularly troubled late at night when I'd have dreams of the terrible destruction in Italy and Germany. Sometimes I'd wake up in a cold sweat, with visions of hundreds of hollow-eyed Germans marching forlornly through the rubble that had once been their home. I think part of the confusion was caused by the constantly changing circumstances I'd been through. In less than a year I'd gone from airman, to prisoner, to escaped convict, and now I was a patient onboard a clean, powerful ship, with people to care for me and to help with the basic activities of daily living. Meanwhile back in Europe, millions of displaced people continued to suffer in a season of starvation. It was hard to make sense of it all, and sometimes I thought I'd go a little crazy thinking about it.

On about the fifth day at sea we got the exciting news that Japan had surrendered unconditionally, which officially brought World War II to a close. Everybody let out a cheer and those of us who could get up and move about went around slapping each other on the back and cheering. It was great to think that there was no more war to kill or wound people, and I was proud that America and the other Allies had won the struggle for freedom.

After a week onboard the hospital ship, an announcement came over the public address system that we'd be docking at Staten Island in New York later that afternoon. When land was sighted, a big cry went up throughout the ship, and everybody who could find their way to a deck moved out to see us enter New York harbor. As we sailed through the Verazano Narrows, everyone strained to see if they could be the first to glimpse the Statue of Liberty. I don't know who spotted her first, but everyone rushed to the port side of the ship and watched as the afternoon sun struck this magnificent symbol of freedom. Chills went up and down my spine. Then, in an unrehearsed celebration, we joined in a ritual repeated by millions of men on other returning troopships as we started shouting and cheering for the great lady of freedom. Our particular ship must have made quite a spectacle to others in the harbor as we stood at the railings in our pajamas and hospital slippers. Some men hobbled on deck with crutches, others were brought out in wheelchairs, and some, who were blind, had to be told what direction to face as their friends described what they saw. As I stood there congratulating a group of acquaintances from my hospital ward, I was overcome with a sense of pride and gratitude and I cheered with the best of them.

Everybody on board was so excited when the ship docked. This meant we could soon go home. After disembarking from the ship we were taken to a large hospital that had been set aside for returning casualties of war. They were well equipped to care for us. The jubilation in the streets was unbelievable and every returning troop ship gave cause for a new celebration. As one of the wounded I was treated like royalty. Army photographers wanted to take my picture and make a big deal out of my experiences as a prisoner of war, but I was self-conscious about the way I looked and really didn't want to talk to anybody about it. It was just too painful to keep those experiences at the forefront of my mind when what I really wanted to do was forget everything that had happened during the war and get on with a normal, sane life. Little did I know that it would be years before that would happen.

The American doctors decided to start all over by giving me a full physical examination, complete with dozens of new tests and x-rays. After about three days of tests two of the doctors came in and asked if they could talk to me. I knew right then that something was wrong.

They said that they couldn't find a crucial section of my large intestine. They believed that because of the extensive damage to my digestive system, stomach acids and digestive enzymes were leaking into my body cavity. It was as if my body had started to consume itself, damaging vital organs in the process. I asked them how they could repair the intestine so that my body could heal, to which they replied rather glumly that while they thought they could find a diet that would ease the constant pain of the dysentery, there was nothing they could do to replace the missing part of my digestive system. I caught my breath for a moment and then asked them exactly what that meant about my long-term health and recovery. One of the doctors swallowed a bit self-consciously and told me that at the very longest I had two years to live. Then he fell silent.

At this news I felt completely lost and wondered what I should do. My first instinct was to stay in New York and not go home—just sort of get lost so that Afton and Randy wouldn't have to go through the pain of getting to know me again only to have me die in a couple of years. Maybe it would be best if I just disappeared. I cried myself to sleep that night worrying about my family and what this awful news meant to us.

When I awakened the next morning I did some serious thinking and praying. I rehearsed in my mind all the miraculous events that had preserved my life through the war, and I recalled the special times that I'd felt the Lord's spirit telling me to be calm, that all was well. I couldn't believe that my life had been preserved "accidentally" when so many around me had died. It just didn't make sense that He would let me die when freedom was in my grasp. I cried out to the Lord for understanding and comfort, and pleaded with Him to remember me once more in my afflictions.

In the midst of this dark moment, when I was alone in an anti-septic room in New York City, He came to me once again. The warmth of His spirit made me feel as if I were being lifted up and out of the bed and held by a hand that supported me and reassured me that I shouldn't worry because these experiences would be turned to my own good. All of the anxieties of my medical condition melted away, leaving me with a calm assurance that somehow things would work out. I didn't know how, and I certainly didn't expect that it would be trouble-free, but somehow I knew that God was with me. That night I fell asleep easily and enjoyed the simple dreams of home and family.

The doctors and nurses were surprised the next morning to find me calm and cheerful. They were happy that I felt better and went out of their way to be kind to me. After working with my diet for a few more days they put in the paperwork so I could go home. They also arranged for medical care in Utah. I thanked them with all my heart and then started getting ready for the long train trip to the west.

Before leaving I asked permission to call home and talk to Afton. She had previously received a telegram telling her I'd been liberated and that I would call when I arrived in the States. In view of the feelings of the day before, I decided not to tell her or anyone else what the doctors had said about my condition being terminal. When she picked up the phone and said "Hello" in her beautiful, cheerful voice, I was so choked up I could hardly get any words out, and tears streamed down my face. When she figured out that it was me, she cried out, "Oh, Joe, where are you, and are you okay?"

I didn't realize it at the time, but Afton had received a telegram shortly after my aircraft had been shot down that reported me missing in action. Nearly a month passed before a short-wave "Ham" radio operator called her from the midwest to tell her that a report had appeared in a New York area newspaper indicating that I'd been captured and taken as a prisoner of war. Shortly after that, she had received another telegram from the War Department confirming my status as a prisoner of war. That was the last she had heard of me. All the letters that I had written never arrived, so she'd been left to worry for nearly eight months with no news. For the first time in two years she heard my voice, and you can just imagine the feelings she had.

When I was able to regain my composure I told her that I was in New York about to board a train for Salt Lake City, and I would be at Fort Douglas in about five days. We both choked back tears of joy and chattered happily as she told me about how big Randy was and how much everyone had been praying for me. I realized then that even in the loneliest moments I had never been truly alone. I had been in so many people's prayers. I felt like I wanted to go to the train station that very minute to start the trip home.

After an exhausting two-thousand-mile train trip (where I stayed close to the bathroom) we pulled into Union Station in Salt Lake City. As uncomfortable as I was on this trip, I couldn't help but remember how awful it had been to be crammed into the narrow-gauge European freight cars, and I was grateful for the commodious and comfortable seating on an American train. As soon as the medics checked me in at the Ft. Douglas hospital, I asked the doctors to discharge me so I could go home. They processed my paperwork in record time, and an army driver pulled a car up to the front steps.

As we drove through the streets of Salt Lake City on our way back to the court of homes my mother had purchased and managed when my father died, I was emotionally overwhelmed to see the places that had been part of my childhood. Afton had been living in one of Mom's rental homes, and I strained for the first glimpse of our house. Salt Lake City seemed so quiet and clean compared to the crowded cities of Europe and New York. Spring was in full swing, with blossoms on the trees and tulips in the flowerbeds. After everything I'd been through it seemed impossible that I was back where I started, and that I was safe. My heart was full and tears streamed down my cheeks. The driver asked if this was the right place, and I was embarrassed when I had trouble replying to his question. He just smiled and said that a lot of guys had trouble talking when they first got home. I'd never had such an emotional response to a place before then, nor since. My heart started to beat faster at the thought that in just a few moments I'd see my wife and family.

When I met Afton at the front door of our small house she seemed so happy to see me, even though it had to be a shock for her to see my emaciated condition. She was holding Randy in her arms, and I didn't quite know what to do, so I just reached out to hug them both. Randy pushed me away and said in his small, toddler's voice, "Go away!" I could see that Afton was hurt, but I didn't know what to do. The only time I'd ever seen Randy was when I gave him a father's blessing when he was still an infant. It was quite natural that he didn't want anyone hugging his mother. We went inside and she put Randy down in his playpen.

Then we hugged each other as though we would never let go. It was so great to smell her hair and look into her eyes. I'd dreamed of this moment a thousand times since she climbed on the bus in Tennessee, and on so many occasions it was the only thing that kept me going. Now, it was hard to believe that all those dreams had come true. We both stood there and sobbed. Finally we stood back and she smiled at me, and it felt like everything was going to be fine.

After a while alone as a family, Afton asked if I wanted to go over and see my family. Since their house was just next door to ours I was sure they'd seen the army cab pull up, but they had refrained from coming over so Afton and I could have a private reunion. I was anxious to see them, but kind of nervous because of my appearance. But I swallowed hard and said, "Sure, let's go." Afton picked Randy up and held him with one arm, and looped her other arm through mine as a sign of affection as well as to give me support. Randy still looked at me warily whenever I made eye contact with him, but he apparently knew the trip to Grandma's house was pleasant, so he was excited to be going there.

Life had been hard for my mother. My dad died when I was ten years old as the result of an industrial accident that damaged his kidney.[2] My grandfather Berry had been successful in real estate, and even though Dad had died in the midst of the Great Depression, Grandfather was able to purchase a court of homes that he financed for my mom. This gave her a place to live as well as a source of income. We did all the maintenance and upkeep as a family, and Mom was successful enough in business to support us and pay off the debt to Grandfather from the rents we collected.

My mother was an indefatigable single parent who sacrificed to help other families in the ward, even though we were struggling just as much as any of the families she helped. It was her nature to work hard and help others. One of the best things about having the court was that that Mom could be home or at least in the neighborhood whenever we needed her, so she was always close to us. Plus, it was good for all of us to have to work to make ends meet. It held us together as a family. The court had been the center of our lives, and even my friends had spent many hours helping me fix things before we ventured out to play sports. As I approached Mom's house all these thoughts flooded into my memory, and I started weeping again, out of gratitude that the Lord had brought me home.

When the door opened and I saw my mom, we just sort of fell into each other's arms. The hug that had picked me up as a child now supported my frail frame, and I felt the old warmth of her embrace. I could almost feel her energy transfer into my body, and I felt stronger than I had in months. When she released me she stepped back, straightened the shirt on my shoulders, gave me an appraising look and told me it was good to see me.

I could see that she was shocked by my appearance, but when she saw my concern she covered her feelings pretty well, explaining that her tears were happy tears because all her prayers had been answered. Next, each of my three living sisters came up and gave me a hug and smile, and then I looked at my younger brother Ben. He was nine years younger than me, so he was just an eleven-year-old boy when I left home. Now he was a healthy young man who smiled shyly upon seeing me. I gave him as strong a hug as I could and we both laughed when he glanced down at my skinny body. It had to be quite a contrast to the football player he remembered from before the war. I was just glad to be there, and as I stood in my mother's house all the familiar odors and scenes that had been part of my childhood comforted me and helped me realize that I was home and with the people I loved.

Before long, neighbors started to come by to see me. It lifted my spirits to know that they cared. Yet it was rough when they would ask questions about what it was like. I just couldn't talk about it. How could I describe combat to someone who'd never experienced standing in a pool of blood on the floor of an aircraft that's been nearly torn apart by enemy flak, frantically trying to help crewmates staunch the flow of blood from their wounds so they won't die on the spot? How could I explain that I'd witnessed German guards kick a man to death while he lay writhing on the ground in agony, while my friends and I had to stand by doing nothing? How could I explain what it felt like to have a German officer know even the names of my wife and son, and threaten that they'd be harmed if I didn't violate my oath of service and betray my friends? I understood their curiosity, but their questions would provoke a flood of emotions that were too deep to visit. I always worried that if I tried to explain any of this, I'd break down sobbing from all the suppressed emotion. Instead I'd just sort of stand there, not really knowing what to do. Afton soon learned to help cover my embarrassed silence by tactfully changing the subject to divert their attention.

I wish I could say that the relationship between Afton and me picked right up where we left it, but that wouldn't be telling the whole story. The truth was that we had to get to know each other all over again. We'd been separated nearly three times as long as we'd been married. One of our biggest problems was my nightmares. I would wake up in the middle of the night, shaking from a dream that I was still in prison camp, or on the exodus from Poland through Germany. The dreams were interactive. If my feet were cold, I'd dream that I was standing on the prison compound barefoot because I had rushed out to roll call before I had time to put on my boots. If my legs hurt or cramped in my sleep, I'd dream I was on the lam again, trying to reach the Allied lines, but could never quite make it. If there was a noise outside, I dreamt that a German SS guard was shooting one of my friends, and I'd lunge at the guard to try to stop him. My usual reaction was to sit bolt upright, breathe heavily, and maybe even sob. Afton was very kind to me and never said anything, except to comfort me and try to help me go back to sleep. I sometimes felt that I would always be a prisoner of the war because it was always part of my thinking.

My experiences had made me quite intolerant and impatient. The first day we went to the grocery store together Afton went to the fresh produce section and picked through the tomatoes, feeling each of them carefully to select the best. Then she'd put them in the basket one by one. I became really uptight and told her to buy the first one and to not be so fussy. I started lecturing her about how hungry I'd been and how grateful Roland, Lloyd, Bob, and I would have been for anything like this. She didn't say much, and put the remaining tomatoes in the basket without checking them. When we got to the meat counter she started to give the butcher very precise instructions on the kind of cut she wanted, and I jumped on her again. She bit her lip, but I was so indignant that I didn't notice her dismay. This went on for a few weeks before Afton sat me down and told me what I'd been doing and how hard it was for her. I was startled, to say the least, and I apologized and asked for her forgiveness. I realized that while my world had changed completely in the past two years, everybody else had gone on living, and it was up to me to adjust, not them.

I was also overly strict with Randy, often insisting that he clean the food off his plate while I lectured him about how grateful he should be. It was Afton, once again, who pointed out that I was much too hard on such a little boy, and too impatient with everyone. It was only then that I let up on him.

My health was a much bigger problem than I had anticipated. I had a difficult time sleeping because of the pain in my legs and stomach. As I tried to eat a normal diet of fruits, vegetables, and lean meats, my dysentery flared up and I started to break out with boils and carbuncles on the moist areas of my body. I had them on my eyelids, under my arms, on my neck, and on the inner parts of my legs. They even broke out on my face and rear end. If I ate anything with grease in it all the carbuncles would swell up until the pain was almost unbearable. Afton and I were at wits' end, so she took me back to the Fort Douglas hospital for treatment. This was really depressing. I was back from the war and I felt I should have been home with my family instead of sitting by myself in a hospital bed in too much pain to even roll over. Before long my condition cleared up and I returned home again. I was hopeful this time, but as soon as I started eating regular food the dysentery came back worse than ever. Upon reporting this I was told that it was in my best interest to go to a special rehabilitation hospital in Long Beach, California, that was better prepared to deal with prisoner-of-war related illnesses.

What a blow. I had to say good-bye to my family all over again, and I found myself standing on a railroad car bound for California, watching them disappear into the distance. It was so disappointing. The medical staff in Long Beach was terrific, though, and the doctors and nurses did their very best to help me overcome my physical afflictions. At times it seemed like my medical problems were incurable, and then I'd remember what the doctors in New York had told me and I'd start to feel blue. One night, I made my concerns a matter of special prayer and the Lord helped me recall the warm feeling I'd received back in the hospital room in New York. I felt comforted by an assurance that if I would be patient, things would turn out okay.

While at the hospital, I met several men who had been imprisoned in Germany and we formed a small group to talk about our experiences. This brought back both good and bad memories, and it was emotionally difficult to deal with them. But at least these former prisoners could understand what I was feeling and how frustrating it was to be back home where people acted like nothing had happened—where there was so much food and abundance that everyone seemed to take it for granted. I was grateful for all this, but I felt so guilty. I couldn't help but remember all the German citizens who were nearly as starved as we prisoners were, while here in America people didn't seem to want for anything. It was a difficult thing to work through in my mind.

The patients weren't allowed to go into town (probably out of fear that we'd eat something that would undo our medical regimen), but we could walk around the magnificent grounds of the hospital to exercise our legs and bodies. There were trees, flowers, and small ponds and streams that made it an idyllic setting. The gardens had been cultivated to create a sense of serenity, and at this point in my life I needed some serenity. For the first time in years I found myself actually relaxing a bit and letting my guard down. It also helped to call Afton several times a week to keep her updated on my condition. In time my dysentery subsided and I started to gain a little weight. After about a month I was cleared for medical release back to the doctors in Salt Lake City.

When I returned home the army said I'd earned enough points to be discharged. That was great news because it meant that I could make my own choices about medical care and about my employment. I appreciated the army medical staff, but I felt that perhaps a local doctor could take a more long-term approach to my care. The army personnel who had prepared my discharge papers also told me that I had been awarded the Distinguished Flying Cross—the highest honor awarded by the Army Air Forces. When I expressed pleasure at this surprise, one of the men looked down and said, "Oh wait, it says you'll receive two of them, and they'll both be mailed to your home." I surmised that I received them for the miracle mission, when I'd helped to save the lives of the wounded members of my crew, and for number 49, when I'd been shot down. The officer in charge also told me that I would receive a small monthly pension of $12.50 from the government because of my medical condition. Then, with a salute and handshake, I was officially discharged from the Armed Services of the United States on August 26, 1945, after serving two and a half years. I walked out of the hospital a free man! Free, at least, from army rules and regulations. But I still had my health condition to accompany me into civilian life.

With an official discharge in my hand I was free to go back to civilian employment, so I went down to the Union Pacific Railroad and presented myself to the personnel department. They were as good as their word and hired me back to a job equal in status to the one I'd given up when I was drafted. It felt great to get back to work.

As I settled into a normal working routine, my life started to come back together for me. I was pleased to provide for my family again, and Afton and I found the things that had made us such great friends before the war were still part of our personalities. Our love deepened and I drew even closer to her as she helped me work through the physical and emotional traumas that had followed me home from Europe.

In time I purchased a gas station that I operated with my brother, Ben, and eventually went to work for Chevrolet as a factory representative, which is where I spent the balance of my career.

As the months passed and I approached the two-year mark of my discharge, I remembered with some dread the prediction of the New York doctors. I still suffered from dysentery and had to watch everything I ate, paying particular attention to fruit and vegetables. But I was still alive and able to support my family. Although I spent several years under the care of a doctor, there were still times when my old Boy Scout remedy of nibbling on some charcoal seemed to ease my stomach pain. I even resorted to swallowing a spoonful of sand on occasion, which also helped to calm things down. I don't know why those things worked, but they did. Eventually the predicted day of my death was far enough in the past that I stopped worrying about it. I don't know how my large intestine reconstructed itself, but with the Lord's blessing and the care of my loving wife, I eventually gained back my weight and strength enough to live a relatively normal life. I still had to be careful. If I ever ate a fresh apple too fast the dysentery would flare up immediately. That is still true to this day, nearly six decades later. It's just one of the consequences of the war that I have had to live with.

The one condition that didn't improve was the pain in my legs. They ached for years and years, and I continued to wake up in the middle of the night and cry out because of the pain. It was embarrassing, but Afton was always kind and patient with me. I received several priesthood blessings for my health, which helped me to endure the pain. After nearly thirty years of suffering, I was blessed by another miracle. I'd been called to serve as a stake president in Cincinnati, and as President Gordon B. Hinckley laid his hands on my head to set me apart in the new calling, I was surprised to hear him bless me that my legs would not hurt and that I would have strength to carry out my assignments. The remarkable thing was that I hadn't told him, or anyone else in that area, about the continuing trouble I had with my legs, and it certainly isn't common to include such words in a blessing. Yet from that day forward my legs stopped hurting and have never caused me any trouble. Once again, the Lord had healed me.

People sometimes ask if I have stayed in touch with Bob, Roland, and Lloyd. The truth is, I wish we had done more. I once had the chance to visit Bob while he was in a hospital in San Francisco after a car accident. Terrible as it sounds, when I saw him lying there with his leg elevated in a cast, I burst out laughing. After all we'd been through together it seemed funny to see him all bandaged up in a clean, sanitary hospital. He laughed with me as we recounted some of the hair-raising experiences we lived through on our escape. I think our wives thought we were a little crazy to be laughing about such things, but it was so good to see him and hear his voice.

I've also visited Lloyd Alburn at his home in Oregon on a number of occasions. On one of the visits he pulled me aside and thanked me once again for "saving his life" by forcing him to keep going when he was discouraged. He had used that phrase many times on our march through Germany, and he wanted me to know that he really felt that way. I expressed my love and appreciation for his friendship as well. I couldn't help but care for a person after sharing a blanket, night after cold winter night, with nothing to keep us warm but each other's body heat.

None of us have ever been able to find Roland. I've tried using some locator services to no avail. I'd love the chance to see any of these guys again. In some ways it really doesn't matter, though, because the friendship we forged walking across Germany was strong enough to endure forever. These men will always be a part of my life, for they helped shape who I am.

Perhaps the greatest miracle in my life is that fifty-three years after the doctors in New York predicted that I would die from war-related illnesses, I'm still here working and enjoying my family. The Lord has blessed me abundantly, both during the dark days of the war, and in the years since. I know beyond any doubt that in times of trial He was there to support us, and I thank Him for the miracles that preserved my life.

It has been emotionally trying for me to recall the events of the Second World War. I lost so many friends. I also saw, first hand, the human suffering and physical devastation caused by repressive regimes, and many of those images are horrifying to bring to mind. Yet I have also enjoyed the chance to remember the men I served with, and to realize how deeply I came to love them. One of the questions I've asked myself through the years is "Why was I preserved and they weren't?" Sometimes I have felt guilty that it turned out that way. An even tougher question is, "Why was I given the strength to help my fellow crewmates survive the miracle mission, only to lose them on our last flight together?"

Truthfully, I don't know the answer to either question. I simply know my life was preserved by miracles, and I have always felt that the Lord had other work for me to do. I've tried hard to be faithful in His service and to live up to His expectations. As I was talking with my co-author one day, he suggested that sometimes the Lord preserves witnesses to bear record of important events, and perhaps my life was spared so I could tell this story now. I like that thought. It feels good to speak of the heroic deeds of my comrades who gave their lives for freedom. The following verse by Louise N. Parter beautifully describes their sacrifice.

> *Honour to the immortal dead, that great . . . company*
> *of shining souls who gave their youth that the world might*
> *grow old in peace.*

In spite of all the hardship we suffered, it was a privilege to serve in the cause of freedom in World War II.

NOTE

1. My oldest sister had died of an illness shortly after my father's death. That experience added to the loss I felt at losing my dad, and was one of the reasons I turned to God in prayer, even as a young man.

APPENDIX
Crew Assignments, The B-17 Aircraft, & Photos

THE B-17 AIRCRAFT CREW ASSIGNMENTS

Illustration by Steven Jensen

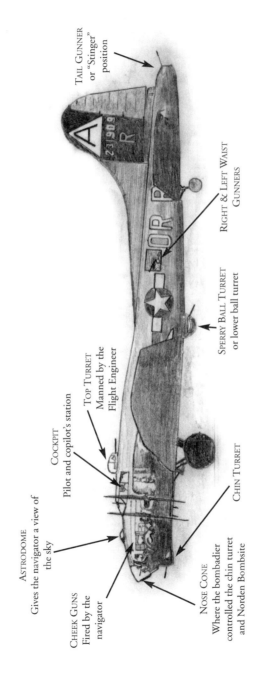

TAIL GUNNER or "Stinger" position

RIGHT & LEFT WAIST GUNNERS

SPERRY BALL TURRET or lower ball turret

ASTRODOME
Gives the navigator a view of the sky

COCKPIT
Pilot and copilot's station

TOP TURRET
Manned by the Flight Engineer

CHEEK GUNS
Fired by the navigator

CHIN TURRET

NOSE CONE
Where the bombadier controlled the chin turret and Norden Bombsite

PILOT & COPILOT

The pilot and copilot had operational responsibility to fly the aircraft. The pilot was also designated as the aircraft commander (AC), which gave him leadership responsibility for the entire crew. In this role he was the one to determine if a mission should be aborted because of damage or mechanical problems. Every member of the crew had to pass a series of rigorous physical, psychological, and intelligence tests to qualify for the AAF (Army Air Forces). An additional battery of psychomotor assessments, including analyses of hand-eye-foot coordination, classified those individuals who could serve as a pilot, navigator, or bombardier.[1] Pilots were in superb physical condition, and their psychological profile indicated an ability to stay calm in even the most stressful of situations. The distinction of earning their wings as a pilot came only after completing flight training and demonstrating the maturity to make decisions under the stress of simulated emergency situations. B-17s were not easy to fly and a wrong decision could scuttle a flight. The AC carried an enormous leadership responsibility, with life and death hanging on his decisions; yet, this task was assigned to young men in their twenties.

There was a difference in pilots. The highest risk takers and most agile thinkers gravitated towards fighter aircraft where they flew two to two-and-a-half times faster than our bombers. They were the ones with the "devil-may-care" look and cocky attitude needed for tactical combat flying. To an outside observer it looked like they made split second decisions without conscious thought or regard to personal danger. Yet, their seemingly intuitive response was really born out of a deep familiarity and appreciation for the capabilities and limits of the powerful machine that they pushed to the limit each time they engaged the enemy. Reacting to an ever-changing battle scene was almost second nature to these remarkable individuals. On more than one occasion they saved the lives of the bomber crews by driving off enemy fighters at a crucial moment.

It took quite a different kind of skill and courage to fly a bomber that had to remain steady while under attack by ground based artillery and enemy fighter planes. Our pilots had nerves of steel as they held to their assigned flight path, regardless of the temptation to take evasive action. Yet, when the occasion called for it, they could maneuver a heavily laden bomber with remarkable agility, pushing the aircraft to its utmost limits to achieve their assigned objective.

NOTE

1. Edward Jablonski and the editors of *Time-Life Books, America In The Air War,* Alexandria, Virginia (1982), 44.

BOMBARDIER

Plexiglas nose of the aircraft with the Norden Bombsite visible.

Chin Turret

The bombardier had to have hands that were as steady as a rock, and he was trained to keep his voice monotone no matter what else was going on around him. His primary duty was to deliver the ordnance (bombs) payload at exactly the precise moment required to destroy an enemy objective (target). For a few breathtaking moments on each flight he used the Norden Bombsite (which was linked to a basic auto-pilot system) to assume control of the aircraft so that he could precisely maneuver the aircraft to initiate the release of the bombs. It was at this moment that the aircraft was most vulnerable to enemy anti-aircraft fire since our speed and altitude were constant and predictable. The Norden M-15 Bombsite was one of the most closely guarded secrets of the war. Neither the Germans nor the Japanese had anything like it, and it was this weapon that allowed the Americans to carry out precision bombing of specific military targets during daylight hours, which, in turn, damaged the enemy's ability to wage war. In contrast, the British flew bombing runs at night, dropping bombs randomly on cities and other targets to demoralize the enemy. While safer for their assigned aircraft and crews, it didn't do as much to influence the course of the war.

During the rest of the flight the bombardier had one of the finest views in the world, since he was assigned to sit directly in front of the Plexiglas nose cone of the aircraft. His view was unrestricted through 180 degrees forward. From his chair he controlled the Bendix "chin" turret to fire two .50 caliber machine guns. To operate the turret, which was mounted directly under the nose of the aircraft, the bombardier would first lean forward and look into the gunsight to estimate range, speed, and declination. Then, using the turret control, he could rotate the guns in azimuth (a horizontal arc), as well as elevate or depress the weapons to initiate defensive fire. Because the opposing aircraft approached at a high rate of speed, the weapons would be fired for brief bursts, since to do otherwise would simply waste valuable ammunition.

NAVIGATOR

The navigator was stationed behind and to the left of the bombardier, as shown in the diagram of the B-17 aircraft. He used a number of sophisticated instruments to determine the precise position of the aircraft, course of travel, time to objective, etc. The astrodome above his position and two windows in front of his desk provided excellent lighting during daylight flights as he spread out his maps on the small fold-up table. In battle he also controlled the two "cheek guns" that protruded from the front of the fuselage with a forward orientation. This meant that along with the two guns that the engineer controlled in the top turret, and the chin turret weapons controlled by the bombardier, we could bring six .50 caliber machine guns to bear on enemy fighters approaching from the front.

ENGINEER

Top Turret

The engineer was stationed behind the cockpit and forward of the radio room. As an engineer, it was my responsibility to monitor all on-board systems, including electrical, hydraulic, fuel, mechanical, and power. I also maintained life-support systems, such as the oxygen hoses and heating pipes. Each of these systems were vital to our success, and in training we had to learn how to either make repairs on the spot or how to bypass a system to give the aircraft commander as much control as possible.

I also operated the twin machine guns in the top turret, which provided defense against aircraft approaching from above, in all compass directions. Control of the turret was married to the gunsight so that I didn't have to lift my hands to control the weapons. If I elevated the hand grips up or down, the weapons moved in sync with that motion. If I rotated them left or right, the turret traversed a similar path. My thumbs rested on the range knob between the grips where I could rotate it to compute the range to target through a full 360 degrees.

RADIO OPERATOR

The radio operator was stationed directly behind the engineer. His equipment sat on a small table that was his main focal point for the entire mission. The radio operator monitored several different frequencies to maintain long-range communication with the base, and aircraft-to-aircraft communication with the flight leader and surrounding aircraft. Once our aircraft passed into enemy territory all external communications were discontinued since the enemy could monitor a broadcast to determine our position, altitude, and range. When one of our aircraft was shot down and parachutes sighted, the radio operator could call out their position to our fighters, if in range, so they could provide cover during the crew's descent.

The radio operator also supervised all onboard communication through the interphone. During battle it was critical that we could report our personal status, as well as any damage to the aircraft that needed immediate attention. In the early models of the B-17 the radio operator had one weapon that he could fire, but that practice was discontinued in later models because of the need for constant attention to maintain communication.

WAIST GUNNERS, TAIL GUNNER, BALL TURRET GUNNER

Left Waist Gun

The remaining four crew members had the defense of the aircraft as their primary objective. The waist gunners were positioned on each side of the fuselage at the midpoint of the aircraft, where they peered through Plexiglas windows installed with a muzzle mount in the center. They each operated a single M-2 machine gun, which, according to aircraft historian Lou Drendel, ". . . was 57 inches long, weighed 64 lbs., had a maximum range of 7,200 yards, and effective range of 1,200 yards. It fired 800 rounds per minute at a muzzle velocity of 2,750 feet per second. The lead computing gunsight on the M-2 was mounted at the rear of the gun breech . . . and the gunner set the true airspeed of the B-17, along with the altitude. The sight reticule moved to compensate for relative speed and angle off of the target"

Early models of the B-17 had the waist guns mounted on pedestals in an open window, but at 20,000 feet the ambient air temperature sometimes goes as low as –50 degrees centigrade, which made this position unbearably cold, even with heated flight suits and heat vents that captured some of the heat of the engines.

Tail gun or "Stinger"

The tail gunner was positioned at the extreme rear of the aircraft. He had to lower himself into a kneeling position where he spotted and fired on trailing enemy aircraft using twin mounted .50 caliber machine guns. This was also called the "stinger" position since the two protruding weapons looked like the stinger on a wasp or hornet.

Lower Ball Turret

The ball turret was a hollow steel globe positioned on the under-belly of the aircraft. To enter it from inside the fuselage the gunner had to go through a complicated nine point procedure. The turret was so cramped that only a small man qualified to serve there. Once inside the turret, the gunner was physically separated from the rest of the crew, except by interphone. He actually lay in a semi-prone position on his back, with his legs stretched out below him, and he looked out of a window centered between his feet. In this position he could fire his twin weapons on aircraft approaching from below, and could rotate through a 360 degree horizontal arc. Because his view was so restricted, the other members of the crew would call out the position of approaching enemy aircraft so he could more quickly sight in on them. It was a lonely and claustrophobic position and so restricted that the gunner couldn't even wear a parachute. Without someone manning this position, however, the aircraft would have been fatally vulnerable to enemy fighters.

As you can see, each crew member of the Flight Crew played a vital role in the success of a mission. It was a job for a team, not an individual, and we each had to be expert at our assignment.

MAINTENANCE AND SUPPORT OPERATIONAL ASSIGNMENTS

The Ground Maintenance Crew
Operations and Flight Command

The ground crew for each aircraft consisted of a complement of ten or more specialists that maintained the aircraft's operational readiness, even when the aircraft sustained severe damage in battle. These men reported to the "Ground Crew Chief." A typical crew included armorers to load the thousands of rounds of ammunition that were expended on a mission, chemical crewmen to fuel the aircraft and maintain hydraulic systems and oxygen for the life-support systems, mechanics and electricians to repair the engines and other onboard operating systems, and metal-smiths to repair damage to the fuselage and infrastructure of the aircraft. Ordnance specialists saw to the proper loading of the bombs.

These men faced a formidable job even when we returned with little damage. For example, the ammunition belt that fed the machine guns was nine yards long (giving rise to the phrase, "the full nine yards") and weighed hundreds of pounds. With more than six thousand rounds loaded per flight, this required a great deal of physical effort to properly load the ammunition so that the guns wouldn't jam at a crucial moment.

The task was even more daunting when an aircraft encountered severe damage. On one mission, for example, another crew's aircraft received 287 hits from flak. Among the reported damage was a shattered Plexiglas dome, smoking engines, leaking gas tanks, and ruptured hydraulic systems. At first glance it looked like the aircraft would never be airworthy again. Yet, under the able guidance of the ground crew chief it was airborne less than two weeks later.

It also fell to the ground crew to clean up the aircraft, which sometimes included hosing out blood and body parts. While the ground crew didn't face the hazards of direct combat, they were the ones that made it possible for the flight crew to do their job and we were dependent on their skill and expertise to save our lives.

There were dozens of officers involved in determining mission objectives, creating flight plans, calculating ordnance loads, etc. It fell to these men to issue the orders that sent the flight crews into battle and often to their deaths. They felt this responsibility keenly, particularly those who had been members of a flight crew themselves. When an aircraft didn't return you could see the anguish it created.

There were also technical and intelligence specialists to create maps, brief us on local geography, and to debrief the crews regarding Triple A, attack fighter locations and strength, etc. When you add in the supply depots that received and distributed food, clothing, new aircraft, and replacement parts, the number of people needed to support an aircrew grew into the thousands.

THE B-17 AIRCRAFT

History and Design of the B-17 Flying Fortress

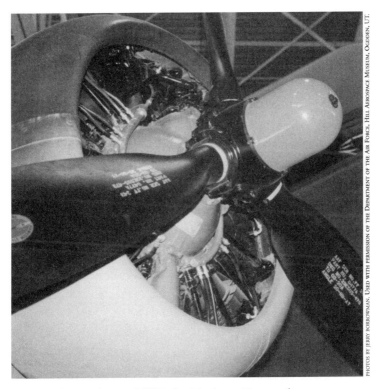

Supercharged Wright Cyclone Powerplants

The B-17 bomber is one of the most easily recognized aircraft of World War II. Its original 1934 design specifications called for a two engine aircraft that could carry a payload of 2,000 lbs. of bombs at a cruising speed of 200 mph with a range of 2,000 miles. Boeing was invited to bid on the proposed aircraft at their own expense, and they took some daring gambles, such as submitting a four engine design, an elevated cockpit that seated the pilots side by side, and placement of the bombardier and navigator in the nose of the aircraft in a position below and to the front of the pilot. This radical design won instant acclaim, but budget constraints and a reluctance on the part of senior Army officials to embrace aircraft as a viable instrument of war, limited large-scale production. By 1940 the government had ordered just thirty-nine B-17s. At the end of the war, however, more than 12,000 had rolled off the assembly lines.

The B-17 was powered by four supercharged Wright R-1820-97 Cyclone power plants, which developed 1,000 horsepower @ 2300 rpm @ 25,000 feet. The cylinders were arranged in a rotary fashion around the drive-shaft to minimize power loss and to allow the engine to keep functioning even if a number of cylinders were damaged by enemy fire. The wing span was 103 feet, 9 3/8 inches and the length was 74 feet, 3 9/10 inches. The ordnance capacity was much greater than the original specifications, allowing the aircraft to carry a bomb load of 6 X 1600 lb. bombs, or 2 X 4000 lb. bombs. The normal payload for a long-range mission was 4,000 lbs. The B-17 carried a maximum of 6,380 rounds to feed the twelve or thirteen 50 caliber machine guns that provided defensive armament to the aircraft.

Cruising speed was rated at 160 miles per hour, with a top speed of 315 mph. The ceiling was 36,400 feet. When the B-17 was first previewed for the public at its home base in Seattle, Washington, one of the area reporters, Richard L. Williams of the Seattle Daily Times, gazed in awe at the massive defensive armament bristling from every conceivable position on the aircraft, which prompted him to dub the new aircraft a "15-ton flying fortress." Boeing loved this description and immediately began to identify their new bomber as a Flying Fortress in all their communications about the aircraft.

References:

Lou Drendel. *Walk Around Boeing B-17G Flying Fortress,* Copyright 1998, Squadron/Signal Publications, Inc., 27.

Fly Past Magazine, B-17 Flying Fortress special edition, (July 1999). Key Publishing Ltd., P.O. Box 100, Stamford, Lines, PE91XQ. UK

Illustrations by Steven Jensen, Photos by Jerry Borrowman.

Joe's training crew at the Curtiss Wright flight engineer training school in Long Beach, California, 1943. (Joe is the second man from the right.)

Joe (on the right) and an associate. Mountains of Foggia, Italy, in the background.

FLIGHT CREW ON THE BEACH OF THE ADRIATIC SEA: (Left to Right) 1. Tom Hynes, Waist Gunner. *His injured arm on the miracle mission got him sent home to New Jersey before the deadly 49th mission.* 2. Jack Cook, Tail Gunner (leaning down and forward between Hynes and Tonkovich). 3. Ron Tonkovich, Pilot. 4. Navigator. 5. Dick LoPriesti, Co-pilot. 6. Mike, Waist Gunner. *Mike had a difficult last name that "no one could spell." Everyone just called him Mike.*

Joe on a training aircraft in
Long Beach, California

Joe's Distinguished Flying Cross medal
(he was awarded two, a rare honor)

```
                    HEADQUARTERS
                 FIFTEENTH AIR FORCE
                      APO 520

GENERAL ORDERS)                              3 October 1944
              :
NUMBER    3783)
```

DISTINGUISHED FLYING CROSS

For extraordinary achievement while participating in
aerial flight against the enemy in the North African and
Mediterranean theatres of operations. Throughout many long
and hazardous combat missions against vital strategic targets
deep in enemy occupied territory, though confronted by heavy
enemy opposition from highly aggressive fighters and intense
and accurate anti-aircraft fire, the personnel listed below
have consistently displayed outstanding courage, aggressiveness
and intense devotion to duty throughout all engagements. With
their aircraft frequently severely damaged by heavy enemy fire,
these men have couragely remained at their station, battling
their way through to their targets to aid materially in the
utter destruction of vitally important enemy installations and
supplies. Heedless of severe and adverse weather conditions
encountered over rugged mountainous terrain and surmounting many
other major obstacles that faced them during these hazardous
missions, these men have gallantly engaged, fought and defeated
the enemy with complete disregard for their personal safety and
against overwhelming odds. The conspicuous and extraordinary
achievements throughout these many missions against the enemy
have been of inestimable value to successful combat operations
and have reflected great credit upon themselves and the Armed Force
of the United States of America.

JOSEPH W. BANKS, 39910833, S/Sgt, Gunner, Rumania, 10 August
1944. 340th Bomb Sq, 97th Bomb Gp, Salt Lake City, Utah.

By command of Major General TWINING:

OFFICIAL PHOTOSTATIC COPY

A TRUE PHOTOSTATIC COPY

[signature]

R. W. ECKMAN
1st Lt, Air Corps
Decorations & Awards Officer

THREE AGAINST HITLER
by Rudi Wobbe and Jerry Borrowman

A True Account

*"Rudi Wobbe: Charged with Preparation to High Treason
and Aiding and Abetting the Enemy"*

Thus began the trial of Rudi Wobbe and two of his LDS teenage friends as they stood before the justices of the dreaded Volksgerichsthof, the infamous "People's Court" of Nazi Germany.

Chief Justice Fikeis wore the crimson robes that gave the court its gruesome nickname, "The Blood Tribunal." The court warned these boys that if found guilty, they faced imprisonment, loss of their civil rights, and even loss of life itself. No one needed to remind them that this would be their first and only chance to defend themselves. The only appeal left to those convicted by the Blood Tribunal was to Adolf Hitler himself. All the power and indignation of the Third Reich now focused on these three young men who dared to distribute information they extracted from transmissions of the British Broadcasting Corporation in leaflet form throughout the working-class neighborhoods of Hamburg.

Why would children, barely starting the passage into adulthood, choose to risk their lives to resist the Nazis? For Rudi, Helmuth, and Karl-Heinz, the answer was formed in their devotion to the teachings of their church and parents, who taught them to respect individual liberty and to rely on their conscience in choosing a moral code to live by.

Witnessing atrocities committed against Jewish friends and others who raised their voices against the Nazis, they decided they must take a stand. Now, their naive confidence was shaken by the torture they'd endured at the hands of the Gestapo and by the imposing judges of the Blood Tribunal. Yet, overcoming his fear, their brilliant young leader, Helmuth Huebener, whose intelligence and conviction stood out like a beacon of truth in the oppressive courtroom, faced his accusers with confidence. It was his finest moment . . . would it be his last?